DOES THE

THE *flip·flop* CEO®'s
GUIDE TO HELP YOU DECIDE

"Finding the right shoe can change your life."
- Cinderella

JANINE FINNEY & LORY MUIRHEAD

1st Printing

ISBN: 978-0-9864259-1-2

Editor: Melissa Jackson, Good Girl Editing
Illustrations by: Shayla Roberts
Cover designed by: Melissa Linden Design
Interior designed by: VirtualGraphicArtsDepartment.com

Visit us on the web:
TheFlipFlopCEO.com

ABOUT THE AUTHORS

We are a mother and daughter who previously co-authored a book called **THE *flip flop* CEO®** which was inspired by our own experience of having strongly opposing views about the subject of network marketing. I'm Janine, the mom, and I used to be "the biggest skeptic on the planet" about network marketing. Today, I'm one of its most passionate advocates.

Prior to getting into this business, I spent over thirty years in corporate America working in various sales and business development positions. My daughter, Lory, discovered network marketing shortly after graduating from college. She did a short stint in the corporate world, and quickly realized that a traditional career path was not for her. She believed there had to be a better way to earn an income. She didn't like having a limit on how much she could earn, and she wanted the freedom and flexibility to create a different lifestyle from the one she saw most people living.

When Lory first learned about this concept, she immediately recognized that it could be a way to design the lifestyle she'd always envisioned. She jumped in with both feet. I eventually followed her, and within a year, we were both able to replace our corporate incomes with our network marketing businesses. That was over ten years ago. This business has given us the gift of being able to plan our work around our lives, rather than our lives around our work, which we believe is priceless. Now that we've experienced the joy of having that kind of freedom, we are on a mission to let others know about this option as well.

As a baby boomer myself, I believe this business is the "best kept secret" solution for the challenges many people in my generation are facing; how to close the income gap between what we have, and what we need to retire comfortably. Millions of people in my age group are facing the very real possibility of living another thirty years after retirement. Most aren't able to afford the lifestyle they'd envisioned. This business offers a solution to that problem.

Lory, on the other hand, is a millennial, and exemplifies another segment of society that this business could be a solution for. Like her, millennials crave freedom and flexibility, without compromising the ability to earn a significant income.

Lory and I don't claim to be experts on the subject of network marketing by any means. We simply want to share our experience of learning firsthand that this business model does work. We believe there's never been a more crucial time to raise the awareness of this option as a compelling consideration for those who are looking for a way to create an income without the constraints of most traditional jobs. Today's Facebook, Instagram, and Amazon world has dramatically changed the way people learn about and purchase products. The referral marketing business model is perfectly poised to fit into this new paradigm.

The Guide is a sequel to *THE flip flop CEO*®. It addresses the considerations and next steps for those who want to know things like: how to choose a company, what skills are needed, and the types of challenges and obstacles people can expect to face in this business.

We hope the information in this book will help to *demystify* this topic, and make it easier to evaluate this business in the same way one would any other viable income opportunity.

THE BEST WAY TO
PREDICT THE
FUTURE IS TO CREATE IT.

ABRAHAM LINCOLN

TABLE OF CONTENTS

Welcome to
"The Guide"

CHAPTER ONE

It's Time to Take a Closer Look: What does being a *flip flop* CEO® entail?

CHAPTER TWO

It's Time to Compare Resumes: from a 9-to-5 to a *flip flop* CEO®. How do I know if I'm qualified?

CHAPTER THREE
It's Time to Choose a Network Marketing Company You'll Love: What's important to look for in a company?   99

CHAPTER FOUR

It's Time to Choose Products You're Excited About:
Choosing the product or service to represent

CHAPTER FIVE

It's Time to Look in the Mirror: What does it take
to Succeed in this Business?

CAREER COMPARISONS

A *flip flop* CEO® Compared to:

FOREWORD

Probably the only thing stopping you from living the life you love is your paradigm. Your paradigm is your current way of thinking – your habitual way of acting, which is creating the life that you are presently experiencing. When you change your paradigm, you change your results. "The Guide" will help you make one of the biggest paradigm shifts of your life, by walking you through all of the reasons why network marketing is such a brilliant business model to live your dream.

Here are points to look at closely if you choose to begin a network marketing business:

1. Make sure you are joining a good company with strong leadership.
2. Make certain the company has a good product, a product you are proud to represent.
3. Make certain the person signing you up has the talent, experience and desire to properly train you. And if they don't, ask to speak to their upline and ask them if they will properly launch you in the business

Network marketing is a tremendous way to get into business for yourself and it is the most moral form of compensation in business today. There is no nepotism, games or favorites; you earn exactly what you are worth to your organization.

Bob Proctor
Public Speaker, Author
Featured in The Secret

WELCOME TO "THE GUIDE" IT'S TIME TO BRIDGE THE GAP

COMPARING 9-TO-5s AND BEING A FLIP FLOP CEO

> **guide** /gīd/ *(noun):* a thing that helps someone to form an
> opinion or make a decision or calculation.

WHY 9-TO-5ers NEED TO UNDERSTAND NETWORK MARKETING

Maybe somebody you know—someone who you'd never expected to be talking about this—has approached you about a network marketing company. And, for some reason, you've got this little voice in your head that's telling you that maybe this could be something you need to consider. But you're torn. You've heard just enough about these kinds of things to be confused, and you really don't know what to believe. You're wondering where to start and how to know exactly what to look for to decide if this is "for real," and, even more importantly, if you've got what it takes to make it work. It all feels super overwhelming, especially since you really don't want to miss out on a good thing. But you also don't want to go down some dead-end road.

Well, you've come to the right place. **The Guide** was written to help people just like you make an educated decision about whether or not network marketing could be a viable option to create some additional income or maybe a completely different lifestyle with more freedom and flexibility. So whether you're still scoping out the scene, or you've already taken the plunge and just want to take a step back to look at what might be missing as you continue to hone your already-amazing-(or-not-so-amazing) network marketing skills, we want to help you with some of the basics to make sure you stay on track!

Just like you, more and more people are starting to see the writing on the wall when it comes to traditional careers, or the world of 9-to-5s, as we'll refer to them in this book.

9-TO-5 = ALL TRADITIONAL CAREERS WHERE INCOME IS BASED ON HOURS WORKED

Whether it's because of job uncertainty, the daunting burden of student loan debt, or a dismal work/life balance, we're beginning to wake up to the fact that the map we've been following is not leading us where we want to go. Now more than ever, we're looking for ways to be more entrepreneurial. We're dreaming about a life beyond alarm clocks and vacation days, but most people don't have the slightest clue what to do or where to start, especially when there are bills to pay and mouths to feed.

Well, the good news is network marketing really is a super cool path to entrepreneurship that's much less daunting than most other options.

we'll refer to network marketing as 'NM'.

Because of technology, NM of the twenty first century looks a whole lot different than it did in the old "bait and switch, garage full of soap, and roping everyone you know into doing a party for you" days.

Aside from religion and politics, there aren't many other topics people seem to have such strong opinions about as they do network marketing. We get it. We've been there ourselves. We're a mother and daughter who had opposing views about the subject of NM, and because of our own experience, we ended up writing a book to bring clarity to this very misunderstood topic. That book—**THE *flip flop* CEO®**—has helped a lot of people gain a better understanding of this non-traditional approach to earning an income. Once people understand the concept, many get it and want to know more. Unfortunately, finding accurate, up to date, and relevant information about the ins-and-outs of going from a 9-to-5 to a NM business, is nearly impossible to find, and has been for decades. And since most of us were taught that getting a job once we're out of school is the "right" thing to do, we've just accepted that having a regular 9-to-5 is normal, and anything else is suspicious. This way of thinking has resulted in many smart, savvy people either not being aware of, or being totally misguided about this otherwise viable and totally amazing way to earn a CEO income in your flip flops.

The Guide is here to help you navigate this new turf.

We believe it's time to sort out the maze of half-truths and distortions, and to start bridging the gap between the two different worlds of a 9-to-5 and a NM business.

If you remember the concept about men being from Mars and women from Venus, you'll start to get what we're talking about.

For most people, the greatest hurdle they'll face when comparing a 9-to-5 to the world of NM as a possible career track, is getting past the way they've been programmed to think life is supposed to be. Launching a career in NM definitely isn't rocket science, but for almost everyone, it won't be a leisurely walk in the park either. The things that make it hard are not the same things that make a 9-to-5 hard.

Going to work with the stomach flu because you didn't have any sick days left is physically hard. Willingly choosing a non-traditional path that's littered with rejection and naysayers just because you feel in your heart that it's right can be mentally exhausting. Especially when everyone around you thinks you've lost your mind. The challenges in these businesses are going to be different. We hope to help demystify the NM option so you can logically compare the two.

"The Guide" will lead you through some important differences and things to consider in your search to find the best NM vehicle to get from your current 9-to-5 gig to the lifestyle of a *flip flop* CEO®. It

doesn't matter if your current vehicle is a Volkswagen bug or a Porsche, this guide will help you find your perfect new ride and make sure you're ready to drive it!

If you're asking yourself, "Wouldn't it be easier to just read the headlines of a few articles…or better yet, Google it?" Great question… which brings us back to the importance of having "*The Guide*"—it's filled with useful and relevant information, unlike what you'll find on the internet about this topic. Google searches bring up all kinds of ranting and raving stories from people who've failed at the business and are blaming it on the game when the player was much more likely the problem. Relying on input from Google sources to find accurate information about NM is like accepting advice about lucrative careers from the Mafia. Would you really put your faith in a Google search for insights about any controversial topic and expect to find a consensus? Why would you let someone else's experience color your decision unless you're sure you can trust the source. We're just sayin', you might want to check out the credentials of those you're listening to before you turn your future over to them.

No matter what your "stage" in life—Gen X, millennial, baby boomer, or somewhere in between—if you're looking for a solution to create a plan B, devise a corporate exit strategy, supplement an under-funded retirement account, or just create additional income to live more comfortably, you owe it to yourself to learn more about a NM "Business in a Box" and whether it could be the right fit for you.

A NETWORK MARKETING BUSINESS IN A BOX IS—GUESS WHAT—A BUSINESS THAT ARRIVES IN A BOX. IT'S LIKE A DO IT YOURSELF VIRTUAL FRANCHISE KIT, BUT WITHOUT THE BIG PRICE TAG AND FINANCIAL RISK TYPICALLY ASSOCIATED WITH FRANCHISES.

Let's start by clarifying what we mean by a Network Marketing Business in a Box. Even though that's not the way most people refer to it, that's pretty much what we think a network marketing business looks like: a business that usually arrives on your doorstep— in a box. So for the sake of simplicity, that's the nickname we're giving it and the way we'll refer to it in the book. It's actually a pretty cool concept when you think about it. For

BUSINESS IN A BOX = NETWORK MARKETING BUSINESS

those who've dreamed of owning your own internet business—but thought you'd missed the boat—this business is for you.

You can finally tear up all those sticky notes, take off that annoying thinking cap, and step away from the drawing board, because unlike most other start-ups, you don't need to come up with your own "great idea" to get going.

Now that the pressure is off, let's pause for a moment to collectively breathe a sigh of relief and take a closer look at why we think this whole thing is so cool. Picture, if you will, an instant business that's sorta like the Energizer Bunny: It's already assembled and ready to go, it just needs the battery, and *you*, my friend, are the battery.

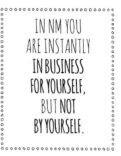

IN NM YOU ARE INSTANTLY IN BUSINESS FOR YOURSELF, BUT NOT BY YOURSELF.

COMPARING A 9-TO-5 TO A NM "BUSINESS IN A BOX"

Before we dive into what it takes to go from your 9-to-5 to a Business in a Box, let's talk about one of the most important differences that's critical to understand between a job and a NM Business.

first: how you're paid. (we know ...it's our favorite part, too.)

DIFFERENCE #1 BETWEEN A 9-TO-5 AND A BUSINESS IN A BOX: HOW YOU GET PAID

STREAMS OF INCOME	
Employee **Core Value:** Security Looking for low risk	**B**ig Business Owner **Core Value:** Efficient Teamwork Can leave job and still get paid
Small Business Owners (Self Employed) **Core Value:** Independence Responsible for Success	**I**nvestor **Core Value:** Financial Freedom Money working for them rather than people working for them
(95% of the population) Trading time for money	**(5% of the population)** Earn money with or without you

A NM BUSINESS IN A BOX = VEHICLE TO FREEDOM
FREEDOM = HAVING BOTH MONEY AND TIME
HIGH INCOME PEOPLE = HAVE MONEY, NO TIME TO ENJOY IT
LOW INCOME PEOPLE = HAVE TIME, NO MONEY TO ENJOY IT

Paychecks are payment for your time spent working.
9-to-5s = Trading your time for money

The previous chart shows the four main categories that most folks fall into when it comes to earning an income. 95% of Americans are in the two quadrants on the left side of the chart. The top left quadrant is the employee category. This is where the majority of people fall. Most adults have been an employee at some point in their lives. Being an employee offers an option to earn an income that is available to most people. As an employee, you have a boss. You know what is expected of you, you work for an agreed upon salary, and you trade your time for a paycheck. The lower left quadrant includes those who are self-employed/small business owners. Usually those with a desire for independence and the freedom to control their own schedule and income are attracted to this type of work. Professionals like doctors and attorneys would be in this category. It would also include those who are self-employed, such as hair stylists, real estate agents, and contractors. Owners of any type of small business or franchise would also fall into this category. Although most people don't usually look at it this way: professionals, the self-employed, and small business owners basically "own their own job". Both categories on the left side of the chart include work that involves "trading time for a paycheck". And, while the amount each person earns can vary from $10 an hour to thousands of dollars per hour, the "catch" is still the same. If they don't put in the time, they don't receive a paycheck.

The right side of the chart shows two other categories that the remaining 5% of the population typically falls into. The income from the right side is passive income. Passive income is very different because it's earned without the normal exchange of time for money. This type of income comes from owning a large business of some kind that can be run by other people. The owners of these kinds of businesses no longer need to show up for work to get paid. They've created a residual income stream from their initial efforts. Their business now makes money for them. People like, Oprah Winfrey, Martha Stewart, Estee Lauder or Rachael Ray are a few well known examples of businesses that fall into this category. The lower right hand section of the chart represents another group of people who have created residual income. These are investors and inventors. Investors earn an income by investing their money in real estate, the stock market, or some other type of endeavor that makes money for them. Inventors, authors, song writers, and movie stars also fall into this passive income category, because they are paid a royalty for work they've already completed.

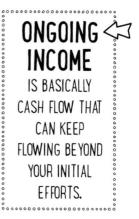

ONGOING INCOME IS BASICALLY CASH FLOW THAT CAN KEEP FLOWING BEYOND YOUR INITIAL EFFORTS.

COLD HARD FACTS ABOUT PASSIVE INCOME

Investments in real estate, stock portfolios, or just about any other income generating asset, unfortunately, come with one small problem for most people: you have to have money to make money. And, do you know how much real estate you'd have to own to earn $5,000 a month? Let us help you with the math. The answer is about a cool million in real estate equity — and that's with a 6% return, which as we all well know, isn't always that easy to come by.

Okay, what about a good old fashioned savings account. Compounding interest on a savings account works in the same way as being a real estate tycoon — at least it does for peeps who are smart enough to put money into savings when they're young. Those go-getters just might accumulate enough wealth to earn some nice monthly interest on their savings. But the problem is that most young people don't do this. Now you know why Grandma was always encouraging you to save your birthday money! The bottom line with savings is that to earn residual income from interest, you have to have a lot of money just sitting in a bank account that you can't touch. And, as many baby boomers have been finding out the hard way, the amount you can earn on a savings account can fluctuate so much that it's hard to know what sort of return you can realistically count on, especially these days.

This chart reflects how ongoing income is created from a traditional savings account.

AT A 5% INTEREST RATE

Amount needed in the bank to earn $200/month	⇨	$48,000.00
Amount needed in the bank to earn $500/month	⇨	$144,000.00
Amount needed in the bank to earn $1,000/month	⇨	$240,000.00
Amount needed in the bank to earn $5,000/month	⇨	$1,200,000.00
Amount needed in the bank to earn $10,000/month	⇨	$2,400,000.00

IT'S USUALLY THOSE WHO'VE PASSED THE AGE OF HAVING ENOUGH TIME TO ACCUMULATE A SIZABLE SAVING ACCOUNT WHO ACTUALLY SEE THE IMPORTANCE OF DOING SO.

Of course, there are those other options for earning passive income, but let's be honest – what are your chances of inventing the next post-it-note, writing a bestselling book or song? Becoming a famous actor, rock star, or athlete? Well, if your answers are "not so good," the good news is that at least you're reading *The Guide*, which puts you way ahead of most people.

Understanding these basic concepts of earning an income is a pretty important topic, right? So, why aren't we teaching more about this stuff in school? The old paradigm of working at the same job for 40 years to receive a pension ended a long time ago. And yet, how many people have created an "exit plan" from the proverbial hamster wheel of going to a job every day? It's easy to see from this simple chart, that if you want time freedom (the ability to earn an income without having to go to work every day), you've got to find a way to get over to the right side of the chart, where you can start earning passive income.

> A NM BUSINESS IN A BOX PROVIDES THE OPPORTUNITY TO BUILD AN ASSET, LIKE HAVING A SAVINGS ACCOUNT, OWNING REAL ESTATE, OR STOCKS. THIS KIND OF INCOME IS VERY DIFFERENT FROM A 9-TO-5 PAYCHECK.

Since creating ongoing income is totally different than what we're used to with a 9-to-5, understanding the distinction is super important. Most people are accustomed to trading their time for a paycheck, and working for a salary, rather than on straight commissions. The reason a lot of people quit their NM business too soon is because they don't always see the results of their efforts immediately. They put in a lot of work without seeing a paycheck, and because they're used to being paid for their effort, they give up. They think they'd be better off with a job where at least they earn some kind of compensation for their time. But it's impossible to create true freedom as long as you stay in that scenario.

The NM model gives ordinary people a way to have access to the right side of the chart and earn residual income. A Business in a Box gives you the chance to build a business that will continue to pay you long after you do the initial work. Instead of working for a paycheck, you're earning the ability to make an income without having to trade time for money. And, thankfully, a NM biz can be built at any stage of life. It's sort of like a "sweat equity" savings or retirement account for those who are facing the reality of needing a "supplemental income plan", sooner rather than later. Hello, baby boomers.

Let's face it; most people are not very good at "delayed gratification". That's why it's important to have realistic expectations as you enter this new playing field of NM. This biz works much like planting a garden. A lot of effort happens before you're munching on a carrot. First the soil must be prepared. Then the seeds are planted. Subsequently, given the proper amount of water, sunlight, and time, your garden has lots of frilly green leaves poking out of the ground with a bunny treat on the other end. No one expects to plant a seed today and be eating a carrot tomorrow.

Hopefully, this garden analogy helps make the point about how essential it is to have the right expectations of your Business in a Box right from the start. To help you determine the time commitment to reach your goals, you'll want to talk to someone

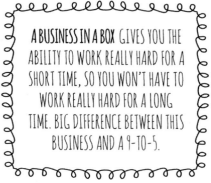

A BUSINESS IN A BOX GIVES YOU THE ABILITY TO WORK REALLY HARD FOR A SHORT TIME, SO YOU WON'T HAVE TO WORK REALLY HARD FOR A LONG TIME. BIG DIFFERENCE BETWEEN THIS BUSINESS AND A 9-TO-5.

who can direct you to the average incomes for the company and help you discern exactly what's involved to earn them. This is normally one of the first conversations you'll have with the person bringing you into the NM fold, which would usually be your sponsor. We'll discuss more about the role of your sponsor in chapter two. And we'll go into more details about pay plans in chapter three.

NM REQUIRES PUSHING THROUGH THE HARD WORK IN THE BEGINNING, TO REAP THE REWARDS LATER

THE JOB DESCRIPTION OF AN NMer:

- Uses the products/service.
- Shares the products/service with others.
- Finds a few others to do the same thing.
- Is a spokesperson for a company and products that they love!
- Teaches, coaches, and mentors those they sponsor.

IF NM IS SUCH A GREAT OPPORTUNITY TO EARN PASSIVE INCOME, WHY ISN'T EVERYBODY I KNOW ALREADY DOING THIS?

The biggest reason even more people aren't doing NM yet, is because most still haven't woken up to the fact that creating passive income is something we all need. It's the only way—short of winning the lottery or inheriting a bunch of money—to make an exit from going to work every day. A second big reason that more people haven't discovered NM yet, is that to most people (maybe even you), a low-cost, low-risk, turn-key business that allows you to plan your work around your life instead of your life around your work sounds a little too good to be true. A life without an alarm clock or a commute, where you can make as little or as much as you want, and can live wherever your heart desires? It sounds like a fairytale to most people, right? We get it! Remember a few pages ago when we told you this business is hard in a way that's different from what you're used to with a 9-to-5? Here lies one of the biggest obstacles of this business: *Skepticism*.

The greatest barrier standing between you and the freedom to do, and have, the things you want most in life hinges upon your ability to believe that there really is a better way—one that most people haven't recognized yet. Sounds pretty deep, right? What's the big deal with having a healthy dose of skepticism, you say? Well, having serious reservations may come in handy when there's a volcano insurance salesman at your door. But just because something sounds too good to be true, doesn't always mean it really is.

We can't seem to trust our own intuition. We allow other people's opinions to matter more than our own feelings. Think about Thomas Edison, the Wright Brothers, and Steve Jobs…don't know about you, but we're pretty glad they didn't listen to all the people who thought their goals were too big, too bold, or too impossible. Even though others likely told them they were crazy, they didn't give up. And neither should you.

Just because things have always been done a certain way, doesn't mean it's still the best way. Ultimately, if people want to create some new options in their lives, they might need to start thinking outside of the "traditional" box in order to recognize what they're looking for when it appears.

Even though the answer to your prayers may not look the way you were expecting it to, this biz is for real: **a legitimate way to earn a great income—with all kinds of freedom and flexibility—and all you have to do is give up some old ways of thinking to see it.**

You wouldn't be the first person on the planet to discover that something you've been looking for has possibly already knocked on your door. But because it didn't look the way you thought it would, you passed it up. Ever heard that old story about the man in the flood praying to be rescued? A boat goes by and the passengers beg him to get in and he says, "I am waiting for God to save me." Then a helicopter flies overhead, and a voice pleads with him to get on, and he refuses, saying that God is going to take care of him. Then…you get the point.

The fact remains that there are still lots of people who have dug their heels in and are stuck in the belief that the NM model is a pyramid scheme. Ask them what they mean by that, and most can't even tell you. But, for some, the emotion about the word pyramid comes from the common misconception that so many people continue to hold onto: they think NM isn't fair because their assumption about the way it works is that one person sits on top, making all the money, while everyone below them does all the work. NM is actually the opposite of a pyramid, and what we're used to, because there's room at the top for everyone who puts in the effort to get there. In NM, every person has the same opportunity to earn as much or more money as the person above them. How many corporations offer all of the employees the opportunity to earn the same income as the CEO?

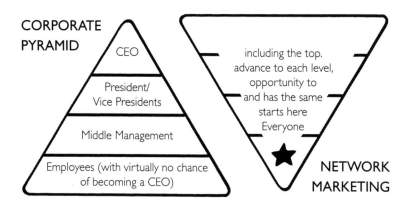

ADDRESSING THE STIGMA FACTOR: SOCIAL REJECTION, HYPE, CHEESE AND SLEAZE

What started all the bad vibes about NM in the first place? Well, many years ago, representatives were actually encouraged to be secretive and misleading when they invited people to hear about their business. You'd get a call from Emily, your neighbor at the end of the block, for a birthday party for her guinea pig. You show up a week later with gift in hand and then *bam!* Next thing you know, the lights are off, the door's locked, and a projector screen is up and running. These kinds of unscrupulous tactics rightfully ticked off a lot of people, leaving a very bad impression of the profession in lots of people's minds.

THE BIGGEST CHALLENGE WITH NM IS THAT IT'S PROBABLY ONE OF THE MOST CONTROVERSIAL TOPICS AROUND, AND THE STIGMA ASSOCIATED WITH IT IS DECADES OLD.

WE'LL REFER TO NM IN THIS BOOK AS A PROFESSION. MANY PREFER TO SAY "INDUSTRY". WE THINK THOSE WHO TAKE NM SERIOUSLY ARE PROFESSIONAL NMᴇʀ's.

Then, of course, there's the thing people remember the most: stories of new representatives being encouraged to spend a boat load of money up front on inventory. Your cousin's friend, Jill decides to join a NM company and is talked into filling her garage with product ripe for the sale. Product that Jill is now very anxious to get rid of, so she resorts to the old "bait and switch" approach she'd been taught, only to quickly discover that it isn't going to be quite as easy as she thought, so she quits. Jill is now stuck with a garage full of boxes and has gone into debt only to own a lifetime supply of soap. In the old days when carrying inventory was required, the person who enrolled Jill had already been paid a commission on that garage full of soap—so they didn't care about Jill and her stockpile, as they had already moved on to the next victim.

For the profession of NM, the downside to any of these scenarios is that there's a complete lack of accurate information about what really happened. Each story, filled with half-truths, gets lumped together with the others, and pretty soon people don't want to hear anything about the topic, so they "throw the baby out with the bath water." The result is that these experiences have created so much negativity; it's made it difficult to discern the truth and have a rational conversation about what actually happened. And because so many people haven't been open to updating their beliefs, those stories are what a lot of people still think of when they hear the words "network marketing."

Plus, because of the minimal financial risk, this business tends to attract a lot of people who decide to just "give it a try" figuring "what have we got to lose"? Lots of people get into this profession every single day, and, unfortunately, their motives, ethics, and qualifications are not all created equally. NM is pretty unique, because unlike most other potentially high-paying professions, where the education requirements, and experience prerequisites eliminate a huge chunk of the population, in this biz, if you have a pulse and social security number, you're in.

In some cases that's good news, but in many cases it's not. Because it's so easy to get in—and so easy to get out—a lot of people do just that. They treat the whole thing like they've just bought a lottery ticket instead of starting a real business. Because of this, too many people jump in without taking the time to understand the business. Then they are encouraged by the same person who gave them the "get rich quick" spiel, to pounce on everyone they know right away. And, sooner rather than later, everyone in their path has been harassed. Their well of people has run dry, and they haven't heard a single yes. Of course, they didn't get rich quick as promised, so they gave up. They walk away chalking the whole thing up as a scam, just like they'd always heard it was. More fuel added to the fire, and the stigma continues.

If you'd mortgaged your house and invested $500,000 in a franchise, and the first few months in business were slower than you expected, would you throw in the towel? Of course not, but because people don't have as much skin in the NM game, they give up too quickly. When that happens, there's one more story floating around that this business doesn't really work.

Another challenge for the image of NM is the hype factor. Any new representative can go out into the community and talk to all kinds of people and say all kinds of things without having any credentials qualifying them to do so. These people end up being a walking, talking billboard for the profession whether they've been in the business a day, a week, or for years. Because of this scenario, there's a lot of opportunity to provide a less-than-stellar example off the profession.

Top all of that off with the fact that the income potential in NM is a lot more than most people have ever had a chance to earn in their 9-to-5, so it's fairly normal to get excited about what they've discovered. They can't wait to share it with their family and friends, and often get a bit carried away. They explain how you can make as much money as you want, on whatever schedule suits you…and it all comes across as pretty unbelievable. So when people in the 9-to-5 world hear about these things for the first time, their walls go up, and they instinctively think their friend has become a victim of some kind of scam. Thus another new NMer has alienated herself, and another group of people have become even more sensitized to this sleazy, cult like thing called NM.

We believe that it's time for a paradigm shift in the way people perceive NM, which is why we wrote our previous book, **THE *flip flop* CEO®**. If you still have even one ounce of skepticism about the concept of NM, you might want to read that book first, and then come back to this one. When you really take the time to understand it, we think you'll agree that a NM Business in a Box is a profound concept.

More and more smart, savvy business-minded people are doing their due diligence, and approaching their NM biz like the best kept secret profession that it is. And soon, the NM tribe will

MOST PEOPLE CAN'T TAKE BEING TREATED LIKE A SOCIAL OUTCAST

have a completely different vibe.

Take a look at the career comparison section at the end of this book. See if you can relate to the people sharing their insights. These are people who are just like you, but have made the decision to trade an ordinary life for an extraordinary one. It's up to you to choose who you'll listen to. Wouldn't you rather learn from someone who has created a lifestyle that you admire, rather than someone who is in the same situation you're in? Every single person who has succeeded in NM has had to endure major rejection and deal with being treated like a social outcast. Every one of them will tell you that it definitely hasn't been easy. They'll also tell you that the life they're living now has been worth every obstacle they've encountered. That's why education about this business is so important. Those of us who are in the profession must become knowledgeable about what the misconceptions are so that we can help to set the record straight.

If you're a NMer who sees any type of unethical behavior, including hype, exaggerated stories, or false claims, please "be the change" we all wish to see. Call people out who are taking part in it. Refuse to take part in the "us against them" mentality. We must stop acting as if those who believe in NM are the anointed ones, and all non-believers are just "slaves to a job" and must be converted or enlightened. This business is simply not going to be

AN NMer's JOB TO PROVIDE ACCURATE, HONEST INFORMATION, NOT DEBATE OR TRY TO CONVINCE, SIMPLY EDUCATE.

a fit for everyone. And that's OK. Once we acknowledge that, we'll eliminate a lot of the offensive behavior people have experienced from many network marketers.

WHY DO ONLY A FEW PEOPLE ACTUALLY MAKE ANY MONEY?

A huge myth that persists about NM is that "only a few people ever really make any money in this business." Unfortunately, many NMers are guilty of causing it. This fallacy is perpetuated because stories about top-income earners are the ones that are most often shared. What is not talked about nearly enough are all the folks who have successfully replaced the income they were previously earning in their 9-to-5, but are doing it without the constraints of having to go to a job every day.

Sure these stories may not be as sexy as the ones about the "rock star" representatives making millions a year, but not everyone's dream is to be at the top of the company with celebrity status. This biz is not the "all or nothing" picture so many people believe it is. Gaining the freedom to plan your work around your life is a lot of people's goal. And that's what this business offers. There are thousands of people in this NM who have created a lifestyle that has given them the freedom and flexibility to live where they want to live, and work the hours and days they want to work, without having to give up their corporate income. Living a life by your own design—whatever that looks like for you—is a huge benefit of a NM business that isn't emphasized nearly enough, but should be.

Who do you know these days that isn't looking for a way to earn a good income on their own terms? So why are so many people searching for exactly what this business offers, but still adamantly saying "no thanks"? Because a lot of people—maybe even you—think they have already tried NM once and decided that it wasn't for them. But what probably happened is that they quit without ever recognizing it as a legitimate business. Timing and desire are very important factors in this business. If you'd tried this biz during college, you might not have had the same desire to make it work as you would after having your second child—especially if your maternity leave was running out and you'd give anything not to have to go back to a 9-to-5.

Many people, unfortunately, were introduced to NM by someone who didn't know what they were doing. Some people probably chose a product or company that wasn't the right fit. Or they were never really excited about it in the first place. What if it was *the experience you had that was the problem*, and not the profession? Did you marry the first person you dated? Or stick with your first hair style? Did you give up eating out just because of one meal or waiter you didn't like? Isn't having the ability to live your life on your own terms worth taking the time to be sure?

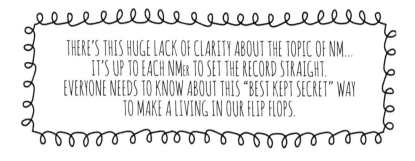

THERE'S THIS HUGE LACK OF CLARITY ABOUT THE TOPIC OF NM...
IT'S UP TO EACH NMer TO SET THE RECORD STRAIGHT.
EVERYONE NEEDS TO KNOW ABOUT THIS "BEST KEPT SECRET" WAY
TO MAKE A LIVING IN OUR FLIP FLOPS.

WHEN YOU CHANGE THE WAY
YOU LOOK AT THINGS,
THE THINGS YOU LOOK
AT CHANGE.

WAYNE DYER

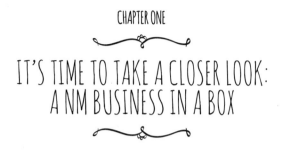

CHAPTER ONE

IT'S TIME TO TAKE A CLOSER LOOK: A NM BUSINESS IN A BOX

Network
net·work /'net,wərk/ *noun*: a group or system of intercon-
    nected people or things
Marketing
mar·ket·ing /'märkədiNG/ *noun*: the action or business of
    promoting and selling products or services, including
    market research and advertising.

WITH SO MANY NAMES FLOATING AROUND IN THIS BUSINESS, ANYONE WOULD BE CONFUSED.

NM BUSINESS IN A BOX = PRODUCTS/SERVICES/INFRASTRUCTURE

To understand more about how to take the next steps
into network marketerhood, we think it will be helpful to start
with a crash course on the ins, middles, and outs of the biz—
and to define some of the terms you'll need to know. There's
nothing more awesome than a network marketer who can
answer questions; not only about their own business, but also

we'll refer to them all as Rep

about the often misunderstood profession they've joined.

NM is essentially a marketing and distribution system that uses independent representatives to get products from the manufacturer to the consumer. Companies that use this word-of-mouth advertising system are really no different from "regular" companies, except for how they make their products known. Instead of investing in traditional methods—like advertising, magazine spreads, celebrity endorsements, and TV ads—they pay normal people like you and me to do the advertising for them. These independent sales representatives are referred to as Representatives, Consultants, Brand Partners, and/or Distributors. We're going to use the term "Reps" here to keep it simple.

When you look at this marketing and distribution model from a NM company's perspective, it is profoundly different and incredibly brilliant compared to what we're used to in the typical corporate sales scenario. This chart on the following page shows an example of how they differ. If a company wanted to sell $1,000,000 of products each month, they would hire, train, incentivize, provide geographic territories, and most importantly, require sales quotas of 100 superstar salespeople. Each salesperson would have a quota of $10,000 a month. (100 times $10,000 equals $1,000,000.) If a salesperson didn't meet their sales quota, the company would fire them. Then the corporation would go through the hiring process, and start all over again.

The NM company flips this model upside down. NM Reps use the products themselves, share the products with people they know, and create a network of 10,000 happy fans—called customers—who each use $100 worth of products each month. (10,000 times $100 equals $1,000,000.) This model generates the same $1,000,000 in product sales per month, but the NM company never had to hire, fire, or train anyone.

TRADITIONAL SALES MODEL VS. NM SALES MODEL

SALES	VS.	NETWORK MARKETING
Full-time	vs.	Some Time
Salespeople	vs.	Customers
Employees	vs.	Volunteers
Quotas	vs.	Incentives
Protected Territories	vs.	No Territories
	To Sell $1,000,000:	
100 Salespeople each sell $10,000 = $1,000,000	vs.	10,000 Volunteers each sell $100 = $1,000,000

REPS PROVIDE THE "ADVERTISING/SALES/CUSTOMER RELATIONS", AND TEACH OTHERS TO DO WHAT THEY DO.

HOW DOES A DAY IN THE LIFE OF A NMer COMPARE TO THAT OF A 9-TO-5er?

A NMer's "job" is sharing the products and/or company they represent—authentically. The process of network marketing happens naturally all the time. Remember the first time you found your favorite designer jeans for half the price? Or when you bought that random gadget from a late night TV ad that scanned all of your receipts so your wallet stopped looking like a paper mill explosion, and turned tax time into a jiff? You couldn't wait to tell your friends, and weren't the least bit shy about letting them know they needed to hurry and check out what you'd found. Why would you? Great finds are awesome and they're so fun to share.

Here's the deal: if you've ever spread the word about anything amazing you've discovered, you've done the very same thing a network marketer does. You probably do it all the time without even stopping to think about how many new customers you've sent to those businesses. Let us demonstrate: you're having brunch with your friend, Lindsey, and you just happen to mention to her how much better you're sleeping since you started taking this new supplement. More times than not, what you just shared ends up causing more people than you even know to start using that product, too. And what did you do? You just told your pal Lindsey about how happy you are with a product that's making you sleep better.

Lindsey then heads off to spin class with a couple of her friends, and when they start talking about their exhaustion from sleep-deprivation, Lindsey shares your story with them. She's not trying to "sell" them something; she's just passing along info that might solve their problem, too. No one in this scenario was really doing anything out of the ordinary, right? The only real difference between this and what happens in NM is that you and Lindsey would be receiving a thank you check from the company that manufacturers that sleep supplement to reward you for all of the new customers you've sent their way as a result of your word-of-mouth advertising.

NM DONE RIGHT IS ABOUT REPRESENTING A PRODUCT THAT YOU WOULD AUTHENTICALLY TELL OTHERS ABOUT WHETHER YOU WERE BEING PAID FOR IT OR NOT.

This whole profession was built around the value of personal recommendations. You use something, you like it, and the next thing you know, you find yourself enthusiastically endorsing and recommending it. Just about every person you know has been a network marketer without even realizing it.

One of the biggest reasons people shy away from NM, besides the stigma, is because of what they think doing this biz looks like. Most think they have to be good at sales. They also think the only way to really build a significant income is to know a lot of people. Or constantly be "on the hunt" searching for more people to recruit. But just as in the example of you and Lindsey, word-of-mouth just naturally ends up reaching people you don't even know.

Let's demonstrate, mathematically, how quickly word-of-mouth advertising can grow by using another example. Let's take your favorite restaurant. You love it, right? So you tell two friends about how much you love it. They each decide to try it, and they love it too. So they tell their friends, who in turn do the same. If this continues, within a few weeks, a few dozen people will be eating at the same restaurant (and spreading the word about it)—all because of you.

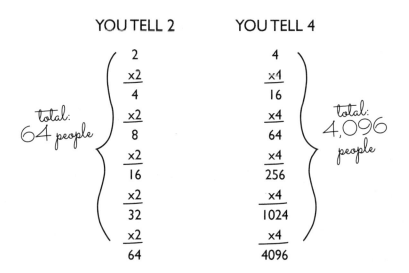

YOU TELL 2	YOU TELL 4
2	4
×2	×4
4	16
×2	×4
8	64
×2	×4
16	256
×2	×4
32	1024
×2	×4
64	4096

total: 64 people

total: 4,096 people

Now let's assume you told just two more people about that same restaurant, for a total of four. And those four each told four with a similar progression. In the same amount of time, hundreds or even thousands of people—most of whom you've never even met—are eating at the same restaurant (and talking about it, tweeting about it, and blogging about it)—all because of you. Remember the difference in the beginning was only two more people who you personally spoke to—four people turned into thousands. That's the power of multiplication. It's called exponential growth. That's the power of this business model. A few people telling a few people, telling a few people, results in a network of thousands! And the internet has amplified this concept beyond anything anyone could have imagined twenty years ago. It has perfectly positioned the NM model of word-of-mouth advertising to thrive.

Exponential

Ex·po·nen·tial /,ekspə'nen(t)SH(ə)l/ *adjective*: (Of an
     increase) becoming more and more rapid.

We want to be clear, these diagrams reflect *exact* duplication. The real world of network marketing—just like everything else in life—doesn't look this perfect. It varies as much as the people who do it. Yet, hopefully, this allows you to see the NM business model in a whole new way. You didn't have to be a great salesperson when you shared the restaurant with your friends. You were just a customer who became a loyal fan. Net-

EXPONENTIAL GROWTH CAN LITERALLY CONTINUE TO GROW ON ITS OWN ONCE IT GETS STARTED.

work marketing is no different. It's about selecting a company you can authentically promote, finding a handful of customers to share it with, and building an organization of people who do the same thing, one small layer at a time.

Rather than being good at sales, you need good systems, strategy, and mentorship. And those are the things your sponsor (the person who brings you into the business) provides when you choose your Business in a Box. You'll get tons of support from someone who is motivated to help you be successful; someone who actually has the recipe for success and is ready to teach it to you. Building your biz still takes time and effort, just as any legitimate business does, but once the foundation is laid, this is a business that will pay dividends in perpetuity. When you build your NM biz this way, you play the game of "follow the leader." You'll use the system and resources that your sponsor uses, and as you talk to people you know, you'll end up with some who just want to use the products, and a few who will see the magnitude of this opportunity and will want to build their own NM biz with you. The best NMers are people who are good at (or are willing to learn to be good at) helping, teaching, mentoring, and empowering other people.

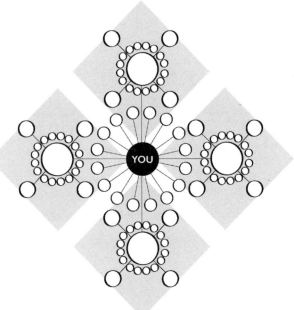

This is an example of your network, including your customers, your four business partners, and their customers and business partners. Every person is part of *your* network, but also the center of their own network...which continues to grow in this same way.

If you needed to find a new babysitter, housekeeper, or someone to mow your lawn, wouldn't you ask people you know who they use? A personal referral is the best source for finding something new. That's exactly what NM is. So why is it that as soon as we label this process network marketing, everything turns weird? It's just craziness, and it's time to stop it!

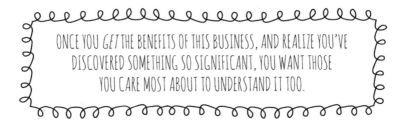

ONCE YOU *GET* THE BENEFITS OF THIS BUSINESS, AND REALIZE YOU'VE DISCOVERED SOMETHING SO SIGNIFICANT, YOU WANT THOSE YOU CARE MOST ABOUT TO UNDERSTAND IT TOO.

NETWORK MARKETING 101: A BRIEF HISTORY LESSON

This business model all started with a guy named Carl Rehnborg who was really into health and eastern medicine. Which, nowadays, isn't that big of a deal; but in the 1920's Carl was onto something. He was passionate and determined, so he took off and traveled the globe, learning everything he could about the health benefits of using supplements in diets.

After several years, Carl returned to the States and decided to start a company called the California Vitamin Company. Things were going okay for him and business was growing, but in 1939 he decided to rebrand the company as Nutrilite.

During this time, he had been racking his brain to figure out a more innovative way to sell and promote vitamins to as many people as possible. Remember; this guy couldn't just set up an Etsy shop, the rotary phone was literally being invented around this time, and people didn't really know about vitamins yet.

So about six years passed, and one day it hit him—overnight he completely restructured the company and called his new sales strategy "multi-level marketing." This strategy was a pretty groundbreaking move on his part, and the company subsequently exploded with profits.

While all of this was going on, two guys—Jay Van Andel and Rich DeVos—joined Nutrilite as consultants. They were two of the very first people to use Carl's new sales model, and they were hooked. The company was growing like wildfire, so they decided to leave Nutrilite and launch a start-up of their own. They set up a competing company called Amway, and in 1972 they bought controlling interest in Nutrilite. Twenty-two years later, Amway took over full ownership of Nutrilite and became what is still one of the world's largest NM companies. Today, Amway has over 3,000,000 sales reps that each use and recommend enough Amway products for the company to sell $1 billion in products each month.

Needless to say, the concept itself works, but that doesn't eliminate the question of whether or not an individual person or company works. Just because your friend's aunt's sister dropped out of her NM business 10 years ago, or because some companies failed in the first few years, doesn't take away the legitimacy of the profession. Speaking of legitimacy,

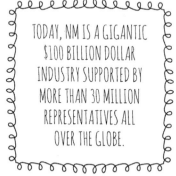

TODAY, NM IS A GIGANTIC $100 BILLION DOLLAR INDUSTRY SUPPORTED BY MORE THAN 30 MILLION REPRESENTATIVES ALL OVER THE GLOBE.

NM has way more eyeballs on it today than it did thirty years ago. In addition to considerably more regulation, today there are trade associations and watchdog groups galore helping to regulate and keep the

NM industry on the up and up. Of course problems still exist, but not on an industry-wide basis. And when problems do occur, regulators are there to protect the consumer.

THE HERE AND NOW OF NM

According to The Direct Selling Association, over 100,000 people enroll in a network marketing/direct sales opportunity in the United States…every week. That's not even including the additional 300,000 peeps who enroll around the world each week. In case you haven't had your coffee yet, that's about 400,000 people every single week, world-wide, heading on the path to start trading their alarms and commutes for flip flops and freedom. And that number only tracks The Direct Selling Association (or DSA) member companies which make up maybe 20% of the total number of NM across the globe. The point is, millions of people from every race, gender, and age are joining an opportunity like this every single month. Millions of people just like you are signing on and investing a few hundred dollars in some kind of dream, whether it's to get a discount on the products they love, earn some extra income, or create a financially secure future.

SO WHAT'S UP WITH ALL THE DIFFERENT NAMES? NETWORK MARKETING, DIRECT SALES, MULTI-LEVEL MARKETING…HUH?

Network Marketing (also referred to as Multi-level Marketing) and Direct Sales are often lumped together. All of these terms refer to a system for marketing and distributing products or services. But there are **some very significant differences** that are important to understand when choosing the right fit for your needs. Part of the reason these different concepts are confused is because companies using these two different models belong to the same trade association. The association is called the Direct Selling Association (www.DSA.org) and it serves as the *watchdog* for the network marketing profession.

So let's take a closer look at what differentiates these two approaches to creating sales through word-of-mouth advertising. Direct sales Reps create their sales by focusing on selling products, which usually are not consumable—like jewelry or cookware—through home parties or vendor events. The Rep takes and places the order, and then usually personally delivers the products to the customer. Because the products are typically not consumable, Direct sales Reps continue to find new people to sell to. They also look for other people who like to sell and want to start their own direct sales business, too. Network marketing Reps create sales by focusing on building a network of consumers—people who consume the products daily and re-order regularly directly from the company. NM Reps build a network of both people who will simply start using the products themselves, and some people who will become Reps and will develop their own network.

We'll explain each of them a little more for so you'll totally understand how they differ from one another.

DIRECT SALES

Products are manufactured by a company and are then marketed, sold, and delivered by the company to the customer through independent representatives versus using traditional advertising and a retail store.

In real talk, that means a Rep buys a product at the wholesale price from the company, and then sells it directly to a customer who pays the retail price. Reps earn a commission on each sale. The commission is the difference between the wholesale and the retail price of the product. In direct sales companies, Reps typically earn a higher amount based on their personal sales efforts. In direct sales there's usually less emphasis on building a network and training a team of Reps, or offering the client the opportunity to shop online for themselves. In this scenario there's less potential for long-term ongoing income. Direct sales is similar to having a part-time job that you can work on around your own schedule. It offers the ability to generate immediate sales, which equates to "right now money." The more money you want to make, the more products you'll want to sell. Direct sales companies usually offer durable items such as jewelry, cookware, candles, and clothing.

DIRECT SALES COMPANIES' PRODUCTS USUALLY AREN'T CONSUMABLE, SO THEY ARE LESS CONDUCIVE TO A CONSISTENT RE-ORDER SCENARIO.

PARTY PLANS

Party plans are another version of direct sales, but instead of selling a product to one person at a time, the Rep usually asks a person to host a party as a way to reach more people and leverage their time. A party can be done in the traditional way, in someone's home or via "virtual parties" through Facebook, Facetime, and the internet. Some party plan companies can be a hybrid of both direct sales and network marketing. These companies compensate and encourage both sales and team building. They provide both the opportunity to earn "right now money" from the Rep's personal sales, and offer the potential for ongoing income by rewarding the Rep for building a customer network, and for sponsoring and training a team of Reps.

NETWORK MARKETING AND MULTI-LEVEL MARKETING

The terms network marketing and multi-level marketing describe the same thing. But the reason we tend to hear the term network marketing more often is because of the bad vibes people tend to get from the idea of someone sitting "on top" of multiple levels of Reps. No matter what you call it, network marketing is still part of the marketing concept where products or services are introduced directly by a Rep to a customer.

"DIRECT SALES" COMPARED TO "NETWORK MARKETING"

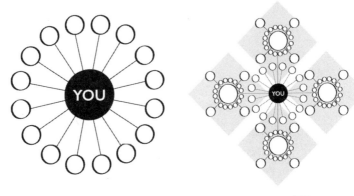

DIRECT SALES   NETWORK MARKETING

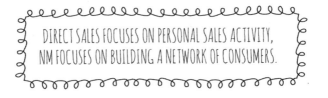

DIRECT SALES FOCUSES ON PERSONAL SALES ACTIVITY, NM FOCUSES ON BUILDING A NETWORK OF CONSUMERS.

The main difference between direct sales activity, and NM activity, is that in direct sales the emphasis is on Reps repeatedly selling products to their customers over time. Usually the Rep focuses primarily on their own personal sales activity for income, rather than on recruiting and sponsoring others. If they do sponsor another Rep, the direct sales sponsor will focus on teaching the new Rep how to sell and demonstrate the products to the customer. They'll also teach them how to provide great customer service. In NM the Rep's focus is on building a network of people who regularly consume the products on an ongoing basis and will often order and pay for those products themselves online. So a NM sponsor will teach new Reps how to grow their own network of consumers and shoppers. They teach new Reps how to share the products and the business. Reps focus on building a network of shoppers who consistently re-order the products, rather than just individual sales. Some of these shoppers will want to join the business (instead of just using the products). So will some of their shoppers. These people are referred to as the NMer's downline.

Let's stop for minute, and explain the concept of a network, or NM team, and what we mean by sponsor, upline, and downline in super simple terms. Every person who joins a NM company must join the company via another Rep. The Rep you choose to sign up with is called your sponsor. Network marketing works similarly to a family structure. In NM, you enter your family structure via your sponsor. So, you can think of your sponsor as your NM mom. Your NM mom also has a sponsor, and her sponsor is sort of like your NM grandmother. Each person up the line has a sponsor, and all of those people are part of your upline, because ultimately, the reason you're with the company is because of them. Like a family tree, they'd be your great-grandmother, great-great grandmother, and so on.

Your main goal in this business is to grow your own family, which is called your downline. As soon as you sponsor someone, you're now their NM "mom" and they become part of what is called your downline. When the person you personally sponsored—your NM "daughter"—sponsors someone, you become her NM grandmother, and when she sponsors someone you're her great-grandmother. They're all part of your downline, and now you've become their upline—make sense?

Your network is your downline, and it's comprised of both Reps and customers who all use the products you represent. You are paid a small percentage—called an override—of all the sales in your downline. When products are sold in a direct sales or party plan method, the commissions on each individual sale are usually higher because the focus in this model is on the Rep's own personal sales activity, rather than building a team or downline.

In the network marketing model, a Rep can earn commissions for their own personal sales, along with overrides on sales from their downline. Overrides are a part of the commission a company pays, that are divvied up into smaller amounts and are paid to the people in a Rep's upline. You are not paid for anything your upline does; you are only paid for products that are purchased in your own downline. Once you've built your own downline, you become someone else's upline, so you are now paid on their sales. In the direct sales scenario, there are far less upline/downline overrides to divvy up because the company's business model focuses more on direct customer contact, and Reps who sell directly to each customer.

If you're wondering where all of this money comes from to pay all of these people, this chart will help you understand. In traditional retail sales, there are lots of costs of getting a product on the shelf that we don't even think about because the costs have already been built into the price, as you can see in the diagram below. By eliminating these expenses, NM companies can pay Reps for their word of mouth advertising. So instead of using Julia Roberts or Catherine Zeta-Jones to be their spokesmodel, NM companies pay people who actually know about and use the products—their Reps.

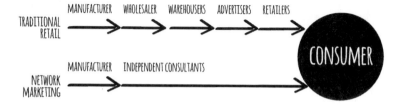

COMPANIES THAT USE THE NM MODEL LIKE PAYING FOR ADVERTISING THAT BENEFITS THE CONSUMER. IF A COMPANY LIKE T-MOBILE HIRES CATHERINE ZETA JONES AND PAYS HER $20 MILLION, AS CHARMING AS SHE IS, THAT $20 MILLION DOESN'T BENEFIT THE CONSUMER. IN NETWORK MARKETING, THE SAME $20 MILLION GOES TO DISTRIBUTORS WHO HAVE (HOPEFULLY) MASTERED THE PRODUCT AND ARE ABLE TO EXPLAIN IT TO THE CONSUMER.

TIM SALES, NETWORK MARKETING EXPERT, AUTHOR, AND TRAINER

When Reps sponsor other Reps, they are paid an override on the total amount of product sales generated by their downline of Reps. Basically, NM compensates a Rep for sales that are generated from themselves forward. This is fair because these are all people who, ultimately, know about the products because of that Rep's initial word-of-mouth advertising. Your downline consists of anyone in your network who you've personally sponsored, as well as anyone who is sponsored as a result of someone you initially sponsored. This includes Reps who are consuming and/or selling products, making them your customers as well your downline.

In general, consumable, daily-use products such as personal-care items, cosmetics, nutritional supplements, household cleaning items, or anything that is used and needs to be replenished have the greatest potential to generate passive income using the NM business model.

A BUSINESS IN A BOX OFFERING PRODUCTS THAT ARE USED REGULARLY, AND NEED TO BE REPLENISHED, PROVIDES THE GREATEST OPPORTUNITY TO CREATE ONGOING INCOME.

PASSIVE INCOME IS THE TRUE ROAD TO FREEDOM, AND A NM BUSINESS IN A BOX OFFERS A VIABLE OPTION TO CREATE IT!

Passive Income
pas·sive in·come /'pasiv/ 'in,kəm *adjective noun:* An income
    received on a regular basis, with little effort required
    to maintain it.

We covered the topic of passive, residual income at the beginning of the book. (Refer to Exhibit A, on page 21) NM is one of the only professions where creating a long-term ongoing income is a realistic possibility for normal people like us. As opposed to a 9–to-5, this business model is set up to leverage your time and energy so that you benefit from your initial efforts (word-of-mouth advertising) through repeat orders, the sales and reorders made by the people you've sponsored, the ones they've sponsored, and so on and so forth. This process of purchasing continues to generate an income for you long after you made that initial sale or sponsored someone into your business.

OWNING A NM BUSINESS IN A BOX VS. A TRADITIONAL BUSINESS

These days, more and more people want the benefits of owning a business (hello, tax advantages), but without all the headaches. And who can blame them! But, unfortunately, as you may already know, options that check both of those boxes are few and far between. Some peeps see buying a franchise as the answer, which it might be if you're cool with the huge expense and risk involved (like mortgaging your house to pay for it), and the fact that in most cases, you still have to go to work everyday. Not quite what you had in mind when you were dreaming of planning your work around your life, right?

NM really is a pretty sweet deal: it requires no product development, research, manufacturing, hiring, firing, designing, negotiating, managing, shipping, receiving, planning, or billing. No lawyers, accountants, patents, website development, logos, storefronts, or office space. And, you didn't even have to come up with a great idea! It's the perfect hybrid of business ownership, franchising, and being an independent contractor. NM gives you all the infrastructure and a proven product or service to plug right into, with few headaches. Plus, you have access to some of the most helpful and comprehensive training around. From product demonstrations and seminars to national conferences and on-line courses; you can attend, join, log on, or replay any time you need info or support.

STILL NEEDING A LITTLE MORE FUEL IN YOUR BELIEF TANK? HERE'S A RECAP:

- **Multiple income streams.** If recessions have taught us any-thing, it's not to have all of our eggs in one basket. Multiple streams of income means that if one stream stops, there will still be money coming in. Whether it's their plan B, a way to pay off student loans, or the answer to supplement an under-funded retirement plan; almost everyone could benefit from having an extra income.

- **Passive income.** The only way to have freedom is to have both time and money. Investments, stocks, and savings all re-quire you to have money to make money. For those who don't have a pile of money lying around to invest, this is the most viable option for most people to build a passive income stream.

- **No barrier to entry.** NM has no age, ethnicity, education, or background restrictions. This is an even playing field. Baby boomers who didn't save enough to retire can put their skills and knowledge to work here, and build an income to retire much more comfortably.

- **No geographic boundaries.** Work from wherever you want

to live. Grow your business from a sailboat or a tepee; as long as you've got internet and cell service, you're set.

- **Immediate income potential.** This is a business where you can "earn while you learn," and you can choose a NM business that offers the opportunity to earn both "right now money" as well as ongoing passive income.

- **Low start-up costs.** If your nest egg looks more like a goose egg these days and you're looking for an easy was to start making money; this is it. The low start-up costs of a Business in a Box will give you all the freedom of entrepreneurship without the hefty price tag.

- **Income based on results.** "Newsflash…the Industrial Age is over"! People these days want to be paid based on their results and contribution, not just on how many hours they logged each week, vacation days they didn't take, or first dance recitals they missed. You heard it here first (or maybe not): jobs of the future will be paid based on the results we create. Period.

- **No inventory.** Long gone are the days of garages filled with products just waiting for buyers. There's no need to have products on hand because products are ordered online, and sent directly to the customer; everything is automated now, thanks to the internet.

- **Flexibility.** You determine your work schedule. Plan your work around your life, rather than your life around your work. There are more and more people searching for work/lifestyle balance than ever before.

- **More efficient delivery.** Time is our most valuable commodity, and gas is expensive. These days, we leave the heavy lifting to FedEx and UPS, which means no more time spent delivering products.

- **Freedom.** To earn as much or as little as you want, work when and from where you want, choose who you work with, and how much time you'll take off. You call the shots; this is your business and it can look however you want it to.

- **Virtual meetings.** Skype and Facetime and conference lines... oh my! Thanks to the convenience and low cost of communication options these days, you're no longer limited to your own backyard; it's easy to grow teams worldwide.

- **Virtual trainings.** You might not know this, but aside from cat videos and make-up tutorials, YouTube has also made it easier to provide and access training for all the folks in your downline.

- **Virtual shopping.** An online business means you can have customers anywhere and they can shop 24/7. Because, hey, who doesn't love the convenience of shopping online?

- Social media. Join groups, connect with more people in your company, and network like nobody's business. Facebook, LinkedIn, Twitter, and basically the Internet in general, all allow us to connect more easily. And that's awesome because that's exactly what it takes to grow a NM Business in a Box.

THE VALUE OF A NETWORK

Your NM Business in a Box is of no value until you open it up and start spreading the word about your products or service, and the fact that you can help others have their own Business in a Box, too. As you've now learned, developing a network of customers is the name of the game in this business.

If you already have a network—or if you're willing to build one you'll own something of great value: relationships with customers. Not just a database of names, but people who know you and trust you. In this biz, your network is worth a lot. That's why it is so important to take good care of every single person who has trusted you with their business. As long as you choose a Business in a Box that you believe in, you'll always be able to share your products, service or business authentically with that network.

People appreciate the value you bring to them. If for any reason things change with the NM company you start with, you still have that relationship with your network. So, if you had to, you could plug your network into a different company and products, and a new Business in a Box. We're definitely not suggesting that you switch companies, we're just pointing out that sometimes changes occur that are out of your control. In NM—just as in the traditional business world—occasionally companies fail, or are bought out, and ownership can change. But unlike many other types of business opportunities, with a NM biz, you have built something that can, potentially, be portable. Depending upon the relationships you've built with your customers, and the circumstances of the situation, it's likely that at least some portion of your network would remain with you.

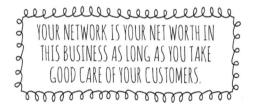

YOUR NETWORK IS YOUR NET WORTH IN THIS BUSINESS AS LONG AS YOU TAKE GOOD CARE OF YOUR CUSTOMERS.

INSTEAD OF WONDERING
WHEN YOUR NEXT VACATION IS,
MAYBE YOU SHOULD
SET UP A LIFE YOU DON'T
NEED TO ESCAPE FROM.

SETH GODIN

CHAPTER TWO

IT'S TIME TO COMPARE RESUMES: FROM A 9-TO-5 TO A FLIP FLOP CEO®

Résumé

re·su·mé /ˈrezə,mā/ *noun:*

A brief account of a person's education, qualifications, and previous experience, typically sent with a job application.

THINGS THAT DETERMINE YOUR INCOME

9 TO 5	VS.	*flip flop* CEO®
Your academic degrees		Your degree of desire
Your education & experience		Your earnestness & excitement
The income you've earned		The income you want to earn
Your past accomplishments		Your future aspirations
What you have done		What you dream of doing

SO HOW DO YOU KNOW IF YOU'RE REALLY RIGHT FOR THIS BUSINESS WITHOUT KNOWING EXACTLY WHAT IT ENTAILS?

Characteristics of an NMer

A lot of people have a lot of reasons why they think they can't do this business, but we think it really starts with your own idea of what this business is all about. Maybe all you really need to do is change the job description from selling to educating, and your title from sales person to teacher, and you're on your way to becoming an authentic network marketer!

If these aren't already who you are at your core, maybe it is something you should aspire to. Your life will be better because of it. Trust us on this.

A Professional Network Marketer:

- **Is authentic.**
  (Psst! That means that you have true belief in what you're representing)

- **Has a good personal reputation.**
  If you have a good reputation, it's for a reason, and it's a huge asset in this business.

- **Has the ability to influence others.**
  This usually means that you're respected, and listened to, because of who you are.

- **Embraces being human.**
  That means ditching the script, the practiced elevator

speeches and the canned 30 second commercials! Hit the delete button on all of those cheesy things, and just be real. We want to stop perpetuating the "ick" stigma.

- **Is coachable.**
  You welcome and appreciate honest feedback and apply it!
- **Educates, doesn't convince.**
  Your desire is for people to have clarity and then to make their own decision.
- **Sets realistic expectations.**
  Whether it's about income in six months, or your progress in the first year. It's important to get clear about the action needed to earn the income you desire.
- **Is engaging.**
  There's something to be said for being inviting, looking your best, and managing your image. People like hanging with other people who look like they have their stuff together. Does that mean you should try to be something you're not? Heck no! Does that mean you should be trying every day to show up as the best version of yourself? Heck yes!
- **Asks questions.**
  Is curious and always seeks to be more interested than interesting.
- **Listens well.**
  You'd be surprised at all that you can accomplish by simply being a good listener.

- **Serves others.**
  It's always in your best interest to look for opportunities to help others, for their own good.

- **Stays in touch.**
  That means communicating well, often, and powerfully. It's staying connected and following through that will set you apart from the rest of the pack.

- **Is enthusiastic.**
  Your ability to show your enthusiasm cannot be emphasized enough…don't hide it, exude it!

- **Shows conviction.**
  Boldly, confidently, and courageously, stand for what you believe in.

DOESN'T NM REQUIRE BEING A GOOD SALESPERSON?

Hopefully, by now, through the examples we've already given, you're beginning to see that word-of-mouth advertising is something that most of us already do without even thinking about it. Remember the restaurant analogy? Take another look at Exhibit F, on page 46. Let's face it: the majority of people on earth don't like to sell. But, most of us have no problem talking about and sharing things we love. So the answer is no, you don't have to be a great salesperson. Being an authentic NMer is about choosing a company and products that you genuinely believe in and are excited to *share* with people. No selling involved.

Let's do a quick review of what the roles entail, for both a direct sales Rep and a NM Rep. If you choose a company that uses the direct sales model, then your focus *will* be more geared towards a traditional sales process. But, you'll be representing and teaching your clients about products you genuinely love. Direct sales Reps spend a lot of their time providing customer service, and following up to build strong relationships with their customers. Developing loyal customers in direct sales is the best way to expand your business. When you take really good care of your customers, they'll want to refer you to their friends. The most successful people in direct sales have strong people skills; enjoy demonstrating their products, and providing excellent customer service. If you decide you want to grow an even larger direct sales business, you'll look for others who would enjoy doing the same things you're doing. You'd sponsor and teach them to do what you do.

If you're building your business using the NM model, you'll be focusing more on creating a network of consumers. You'll be sharing the business and the products with people you know, and as you do this, you'll find some people who are just interested in the products, and a few who are interested in sharing the products with their friends and building a NM business of their own.

You'll teach your customers how they can get their products sent to them directly from the company automatically, or by ordering them online themselves. You'll be teaching those who decide to build a business how to follow a system. They will become leaders of their own teams, and will join you in doing the same thing you've done. Sincerity, honesty, and genuinely caring about others—*rather than selling*—is key to success in this profession.

If you aren't already; you'll want to become really good at listening to what others need. That's the only way to determine if this business might provide a solution for someone. Most people you know—and will get to know—aren't going to lead themselves into a great NM business. There's just too much misunderstanding and mistrust about this concept still floating around. So it'll be up to you to help people connect the dots between what you're doing and what they need. When you take the time to listen, you'll find lots of folks need a second income, a plan B, a back-up-plan, or just a way to be able to afford to send their kids to camp. You're the one who sees what this business has to offer, so you're the one who knows if it could be a way for them to achieve what they want. You just have to be able to paint that picture for them.

Welcome to the "problem solving" and "dream building" business. No sales required.

DO I REALLY HAVE TO BE A LEADER?

No matter what your hang ups around being a leader are—whether it's that you think you're unqualified or don't believe you have what it takes—in NM being a leader comes with the territory. Before you opt out and throw in the towel, consider this: maybe it's just the title that's hanging you up. Many of the most successful leaders in NM didn't come into the business with any prior leadership experience. In fact, many of the greatest leaders in history were just peeps who had a vision for making things better in some way and enjoyed serving others.

You might just want to consider the possibility that for you, becoming a great leader will happen as a result of who you are, and what you authentically bring out in others. Because leadership in this business simply means helping other people succeed. Shoot! No wonder people with backgrounds in serving others—like teachers, coaches, and nurses—really thrive in NM.

Okay, so what does a leader actually do once they've attracted people who recognize the brilliance of a Business in a Box? Leadership is simply the ability to lead people to do things, go places, and become someone they wouldn't have

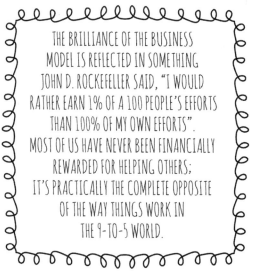

THE BRILLIANCE OF THE BUSINESS MODEL IS REFLECTED IN SOMETHING JOHN D. ROCKEFELLER SAID, "I WOULD RATHER EARN 1% OF A 100 PEOPLE'S EFFORTS THAN 100% OF MY OWN EFFORTS". MOST OF US HAVE NEVER BEEN FINANCIALLY REWARDED FOR HELPING OTHERS; IT'S PRACTICALLY THE COMPLETE OPPOSITE OF THE WAY THINGS WORK IN THE 9-TO-5 WORLD.

otherwise become on their own. And leaders are able to do all of that by holding a crystal-clear vision and communicating it in a way that it sticks like glue in the forefront of our hearts and minds. The cool thing about this biz is that you'll have lots of role models all around you to learn from. Their stories will inspire you to become more than you may have ever dreamed possible.

A leader's actions always back up their words; they have the integrity to be who they say they are, and to share themselves wholly and authentically—fears and weaknesses. A great leader will always listen so you feel heard; not necessarily agreed with, but always heard and honored. They inspire us to do things that, if left to our own thinking, we would consider unreasonable, impossible, or just plain ridiculous. A good leader can teach what to do, how to do it, why to do it, and help us figure out the stuff that has us stuck. They ask the right questions to provoke new thinking about how to remove fears and limiting beliefs. Think about who you know who is a natural leader, even if they've never *officially* been in that kind of position before. Maybe she's a Girl Scout leader, or the mom whose son sold the most candy bars for the PTA fundraiser. Or maybe that person who's first in the school drop-off line every day, looking like a million bucks as she heads off to the office. Maybe she'd rather be sporting yoga clothes than the suits she wears every day. (She might look pretty good in flip flops instead of high heels). This is a business that's all about attracting people who are better than you are. Attracting awesome leaders to your business will ultimately determine how much you earn, and how long you'll sustain it.

DO I REALLY HAVE TO BE A COACH?

Coaching and empowering others are important components of

a NM leader's role. The good news is that by being coached yourself, you'll be learning how to coach others. A willingness to be coached is just part of growing a NM business. Unlike the 9-to-5 world, no one comes into this with their degree in NM and twenty years of experience under their belt. Being coachable means you're willing to learn the nuances, accept feedback, and apply it. Like we've said before: no one else is going to do your business for you. The natural first step in growing your business is to learn from someone who's successful and wants to see you succeed too. Being coached isn't about being a doormat; it's about learning how to work smarter.

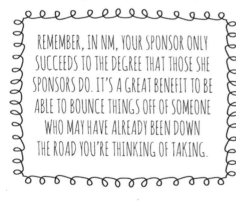

REMEMBER, IN NM, YOUR SPONSOR ONLY SUCCEEDS TO THE DEGREE THAT THOSE SHE SPONSORS DO. IT'S A GREAT BENEFIT TO BE ABLE TO BOUNCE THINGS OFF OF SOMEONE WHO MAY HAVE ALREADY BEEN DOWN THE ROAD YOU'RE THINKING OF TAKING.

This doesn't mean you shouldn't follow your own instincts—or do things that don't feel authentic to you—it simply means being open to exploring tried-and-true approaches, even if they seem counterintuitive at first. If what you're being encouraged to do isn't working for you, check out what other successful leaders around you are doing. This business is like anything else; there are lots of different ways to accomplish the same outcome, so find the things that most resonate with you.

As a sponsor, it's your job to help the peeps you've sponsored be successful. Approach this powerfully, but not forcefully. You're not in the business of hounding anyone to do anything. Believe us, it definitely doesn't work to try dragging someone along. Your success in NM is directly tied to how good you are at bringing out the best in others. There's nothing good about hounding and dragging. If you ever feel lost or uncertain, make sure to head straight to your sponsor or someone in your upline and ask them for help. Empower your Reps to do the same by encouraging them to let you know what they need from you. It's important that they take responsibility for asking for your help if they're not sure what to do.

YOUR UPLINE'S RELATIONSHIP WITH AND RESPONSIBILITY TO YOU:

here's a quick guide to the roles and responsibilities of an upline and downline:

Your upline is there to help you understand what you need to know to become successful. She's there to help you find the answers to your questions. It's up to you, though, to take responsibility for your own business! Your success is your responsibility, not your upline's. Go to your upline when you need help. If your direct sponsor can't help you, ask them to connect you with their upline. Strive to become self-sufficient. Ultimately, earning an income is not about your upline, it's about creating your own downline. Unfortunately, there are a lot of people who blame their upline for their lack of success, which is ridiculous. This is your business. If you and your sponsor don't click, there are lots more people up the line who would love to help you succeed if you're really sincere about wanting to do so.

YOUR OWN DOWNLINE'S RELATIONSHIP AND RESPONSIBILITY:

Be the best sponsor you can be, and remember it's your goal to empower people to become independent Reps, not co-dependent Reps. Ultimately, you'll want to find ways to support others in becoming self-sufficient and successful. Recognize that you cannot take responsibility for someone else's success or failure. Consider yourself the support team to the people you sponsor, including those who they sponsor. They're your downline, so be willing to match effort for effort as a good way to gauge the appropriate time to spend coaching anyone. That means that once someone knows what to do, it's up to them to do it.

DO I HAVE TO RECRUIT OTHERS?
DO I HAVE TO KNOW A LOT OF PEOPLE?
DO I HAVE TO TALK TO PEOPLE I KNOW?

You're not the first to ask and you certainly won't be the last. To be totally honest, one of the greatest challenges in NM is the stigma around the "recruiting" aspect of the business. And rightly so. Too many people still seem to think that NM requires preying upon family and friends. Rather than thinking of yourself as a recruiter think of yourself as a story teller or a vision caster. You'll want to become very good at sharing what your company, the products, and/or the profession of NM have to offer...without being attached to the outcome.

You're probably wondering why, if it's that simple, do people still seem to mess it up so badly. We think this has a lot to do with all the different recruiting methods taught over the years. Couple that with in-experienced Reps excitedly saying all the wrong things, coming on way too strong, being overly secretive, or coercing their friends into weird situations, and you have the perfect recipe for disaster. That combo is what has created the *ick-factor* people have come to anticipate. The truth is that in most cases, the person receiving the information is just as guilty of creating the weirdness as the new Rep because of some leftover memory they're holding onto from long ago. Nevertheless, it can end up alienating a new Rep right out of the gate, and perpetuating the *pesky* stigma.

So how do we authentically sponsor others minus the ick-factor? Easy, and it all starts with communication. Be real. Stay committed to an "open and honest" policy. Convey your feelings, vision, and beliefs. Share your own story, maybe even meet someone where they're at, and let them know you understand how they feel because you felt the same way. Explain that as you learned more, you started to see it all different-

YOU'RE NOT IN THE BUSINESS OF CONVINCING, YOU'RE IN THE BUSINESS OF CONNECTING.

ly. Just don't go into the conversation with the ex-pectation that the person you're sharing with will immediately feel the same way. Remember when we talked about being attached to the activity and not the outcome? Well, this is where that comes into play, because connecting happens when you speak from your heart to someone else's heart.

Don't hound the same people over and over. Too many new Reps talk to too few people, too many times.

The people closest to us are usually the most difficult to share this with. They want to protect us from getting into something they think isn't legitimate. They haven't taken the time yet to update themselves about this topic. This is where using a third party resource like **THE** *flip flop* CEO®. or some other type of business tool can be so helpful in educating others.

90% of network marketers are introduced to their opportunity by someone they know, but in most cases it takes a lot more than the first exposure to the info for the person to become interested. Think of this in terms of dating. You probably wouldn't want to marry someone who proposed to you on the first date. Or, if someone offered you a yummy piece of your favorite dessert, it would look a lot better if you were hungry than if you'd just finished a big feast.

You've got to start somewhere, right? But where? Let's go back to the examples we've already given. Who would you tell about a great movie, book, or restaurant you've discovered? This doesn't have to be any different than what you're already doing. More than likely, the things you love the most about your products and/or business are the same things someone else like you would dig about them too. When you're talking to someone who shares a problem that needs some kind of solution, let the person know about your experience with the products or the business, and offer a way for them to find out if it could benefit them as well. You're really looking for anyone who your products (or business) could be a solution for. If you just stay focused on helping *others*, you won't go wrong.

Remember, NM isn't about you *needing* to find hundreds of people yourself. You're looking for a few people who are looking for you, too. They're looking for some kind of solution. If your products or a Business in a Box might provide their solution, simply share that...without any attachment to the outcome. If you ever start feeling desperate to *find* people, rather than like you've got a gift to give people, take a step back and look at your belief. Something might be missing, because if you're building this business authentically, you should be excited to share what you've found. You build a network by genuinely sharing the products and/or the business with the people you already know who would benefit from knowing about either one or the other, or both. If you're being genuine, people will sense that, and if they don't have a need, they may refer you to others who do. If you love your products, and you love the biz, who do you know who might love them too? Your network growing happens organically when you do this business authentically. When you find a friend who wants to grow her own biz, your network expands to all of the people she knows.

Let's say you have a cousin in California who just had a baby and doesn't want to go back to her corporate job. She's looking for a way to not have to leave her baby, and you have a possible solution. You share the biz, she's thrilled, and now you help her share the products and business with her friends. Your network just grew its first California branch, and from there, it begins to grow exponentially.

Remember when Mom told you not to judge a book by its cover? Well the old adage still holds true; sometimes the people we least expect to join our business, do, and those who we thought would absolutely want to join us, don't. That's just the way the cookie crumbles. Maybe you thought your best friend would totally do this with you, but she still doesn't get it. And your cousin in California wasn't even on your radar screen until your mom mentioned that she just had a baby and would do anything not to have to go back to work. The better you become at listening to others to learn more about what they are looking for, the better you'll be at finding solutions to their problems. And, the better you are at that, the more likely it is that you'll have people think of someone else you should talk to.

WHY DOES PERSONAL DEVELOPMENT SEEM TO BE SUCH A BIG PART OF NM?

There's a saying that NM is actually a personal development course disguised as a business. This is because being successful is an inside game. Think about it this way: how you do *anything* is how you do *everything*, so the better you become at the things needed to be successful in this business, the better you'll become at life. We all have traits and habits that serve us, and some that don't. Be prepared for the things that don't support you in becoming the person you want to be to show up pretty quickly. Don't be scared, this is a chance to change your life from the inside out. How cool is that? Plus, you'll have the chance to get lots of practice every day on changing the things that may have been holding you back in other areas, too.

This is a relationship business, so the more you know about yourself, the better you'll relate to your customers and your team and, let's face it, everyone else in your life.

CAN INTROVERTS DO THE BUSINESS TOO?

A common assumption is that an extrovert is the best type of person for this business. But this isn't necessarily true. Even if you're not outgoing and gregarious, you can still form meaningful relationships and communicate your ideas. Introverts often eliminate themselves from NM because they aren't good at initiating conversations, which is unfortunate, because there are two equally important aspects of this business. One is talking to people, but the other is *listening* to people. Introverts are often much better listeners. Self-understanding is the key here. Figure out what your strengths are as an introvert and then use that knowledge to market your products and business opportunity in a way that feels most authentic to you. You don't have to put up a false front or try to be someone you're not to be successful in this business. Don't put that unnecessary pressure on yourself. The important thing to remember is that you don't have to be someone who is completely different from you. Find a way of sharing the business that feels exciting. That will allow you to be confident and authentic, and people will appreciate that about you.

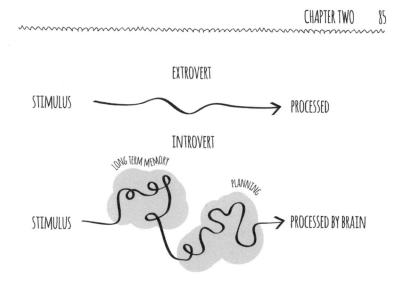

NM FOR INTROVERTS: A 5 MINUTE GUIDE

- **Get intentional about the peeps you'd like to meet**

  You might identify specific people like chiropractors or trainers, who could be a good fit for your products and/or biz. Jot down ideas about how and where you can meet them. Start thinking about what it is that you'd like to share with them. Create a list of words or phrases that describe the people you want to meet. Words like caring, positive, kind, helpful, and honest. You're describing the perfect candidate for your business. By doing this, you're training your brain to recognize them and even attract them into your life.

- **Maximize those resources**

  Even if your preference is not to have any face-to-face contact, NM can still work for you if you find the right internet marketing techniques. The internet has such a wide reach; you can connect with potentially thousands of people with your product or business opportunity. Find resources to learn about this from people who have done it successfully. Just make sure you are compliant with your company's policies and procedures about what you can and cannot do on the internet.

- **Birds of a feather flock together**

  Find other successful NMers who are like you, and find out how they built their businesses. When you're struggling with finding your way of authentically sharing your products and business, it can be very helpful to interview people. Listen for ideas and that thing that is going to make you say, "I can do that"!

- **Arm yourself**

  Spend some time thinking about what you want to learn from others and have a few questions ready to ask new people, like "What are you passionate about?" and "How did you get started in your career?" Think about what you want to share about yourself. You won't want to rely on the other person to carry the conversation. When you ask someone if they love what they do, many times their response will be, "I don't love it, but it's just what I do," or "I love some things about it." This creates an opening for you to be a problem solver for them. Ask them more questions.

- **Opposites attract**
  Consider seeking out people whose energy levels, traits, and skills compliment yours. Opposites can attract and foster very productive connections. Find out what kind of person compliments you.

- **Bigger isn't always better**
  A smaller database of solid clients and advocates can be far more valuable than a huge database of random contacts. If you maintain a list of people who know you, like you, trust you, and see your value, you've got a gold mine. Connecting others who would bring value to knowing one another can be a powerful attribute, too.

USE THE TOOLS, DON'T BE THE TOOLS

One of the coolest things about a Business in a Box is that you're in business for yourself but not *by* yourself, so you have lots of help when you get started! It's really important to let your sponsor and the "tools" help you as you go out and share what you're so excited about with others. In the beginning, what often happens is that a brand new Rep, filled with excitement, begins talking to people, and soon discovers that everything they're saying is coming across as pretty unbelievable. That's because, in some ways, when you really understand this business, it truly is a whole new way of looking at life. Unfortunately, the people who are listening to you haven't had the opportunity to experience what you have, yet. Before you know it, you can almost watch their guard go up as they start to look at you as if you've been brainwashed, or a creature from another planet has taken over your body!

One of the ways we can mitigate the damage that this initial experience can cause is to help new Reps understand the importance of **"using the tools, rather than being the tools."** It's a concept that is effective for many reasons, but suffice it to say that this is one of the most important things we'd like to emphasize in this book. What we mean by "use the tools, don't be the tools" is that anytime the way of describing or presenting something is super important, it's much more effective and efficient to find a resource or a "tool" to do the job, rather than relying on a new Rep to explain it in a way that makes sense. We recommend that new Reps use an objective resource like a book, a video, or some type of "tool" that is devoted to explaining or educating someone about the concept of network marketing, as well as the benefits of the products or services and the company they're representing.

IN NM DUPLICATION IS THE NAME OF THE GAME

So, if real estate is about location, location, location, then NM is about leverage, leverage, leverage. Leverage means investing in something once and getting paid for it again and again. Investors have leverage; their money grows on its own. The founder of a franchise has leverage by building the template for one business, but getting paid for ten more. NMers have leverage because they can teach five people how to do what they do and end up being paid for five thousand. They train a tiny team of people, and end up with an army through the power of duplication.

Duplication is simply the repeated use of any system that allows someone to go out and share the products or the business. Creating a process that can be duplicated is an important component of building a large, successful NM Biz. Think of duplication like following a recipe. If you have a recipe for chocolate chip cookies, and you want to make exactly the same cookies every time, you'll follow the recipe exactly. If you added mint-flavored chocolate chips instead of regular chocolate chips, your cookies won't taste the same. In NM, people tend to add their own "flavor" to the process, and wonder why they are not achieving success. That's why we say let the tools "do the talking for you" whenever possible. This can maximize your time and mitigates the opportunity for failure due to inexperience or lack of skills.

NM is built around the use of systems. When you can rely on a system that has already been created to successfully build a business, your team has a roadmap for success. And the more guesswork you can remove from the equation, the better. The less people have to rely on their own individual presentation skills to succeed, the more duplication you will see. Creating and perfecting a system is a tremendous undertaking, so it's a huge benefit to a new Rep to be able to plug right in to an existing system. It's important to assure that the system is simple and effective, and that anyone can follow it to grow a solid NM business. Just like everything else in life, there's a learning curve. Plug in, be open to coaching along the way, make corrections, and be patient.

Another crucial part of the duplication discussion is something that is often overlooked when teaching a new Rep "the system." It's the importance of duplicating the *engagement* part of the process. Ultimately, engagement is the first step in any system aimed at building a successful NM business. Engagement with others is what NM is all about. So finding a way that will allow each new Rep to say "I can do this" and *mean it* is extremely important. Maybe that includes doing something on the internet, using a business tool, providing a link to information about a product, or creating a perfectly honed story about what spoke to the new Rep about this business. No matter what "it" looks like, the better you are able to do this, the more likely you are to create a large, sustainable, and successful business.

ONCE A REP CAN SAY, "I CAN DO THIS" WITH CONFIDENCE & CONVICTION (AKA TOTAL 100% BELIEF), THEY'VE FOUND THEIR KEY TO SUCCESS. BOOM.

Once a Rep has found their "I can do this" approach to connecting with and inviting people to hear more, then they can follow the team's "recipe" from there. The next step in the system might be to have the business candidate watch a video, listen to a call, or try a sample. After they've done that, they can continue on to the next step. They can keep following the system all the way through to the end, with the candidate either joining the business, buying the products, or determining that the timing isn't good for them right now.

Now that we've beat a dead horse about the importance of following a system, there will be some people who still want to do it their own way. If that happens, it's important to recognize that it doesn't work to force a system on someone. Just remember it's the sponsor's job to empower the new person to figure out what they can do.

Something else to think about is that everything you do is demonstrating how it looks to do this business. People are watching you and are thinking about whether or not they could do what you're doing. Whatever you say when you first talk to a person about the business is when you begin to demonstrate the duplication process. If a candidate sees you handing out samples to people, they're going to think that's what "doing" this business looks like. If they see you speaking to 100 people in a room, they're deciding whether or not they could do what you're doing. It's important to always be aware of that. So if you're ever doing something that they won't *have* to do, it's a good idea to point that out and talk about it.

WHAT'S A REALISTIC TIME COMMITMENT TO DO THIS BUSINESS?

In case you've been sitting here scratching your head trying to figure out just how much of your time it's going to take to build your NM biz, let's break it down. In general, if you're doing this business part time, expect to spend a minimum of 5 to 15 hours per week for 3 to 5 years. It takes time and consistent effort to build this business, just like any other. Prioritize what's happening in your life and figure out where you're going to fit this into your already busy schedule.

For a lot of people their NM Business in a Box starts out as a *commute time business* because so much of what you're doing is connecting with others. All you need is your phone and/or your laptop. You can make tons of headway while you're in your car making a few quick calls after dropping the kids off at school. A great deal can be accomplished while driving to and from work (until you don't have to go to your 9-to-5 anymore). Busy people usually do very well because they know how to get things done in the nooks and crannies of their lives.

BELIEVE US;
IF YOU'RE NOT WORKING
TO FULFILL YOUR OWN
DREAMS, YOU'RE WORKING
TO FULFILL SOMEONE ELSE'S.

Or, if you're someone who absolutely loves what you do…keep doing it! Even after your NM biz becomes a success. The good news is that by starting your business alongside of what you're already doing you'll eventually have the freedom and flexibility to design your own work schedule, so you can work on *your* terms instead of someone else's.

What trips a lot of people up is that you will probably have to—at first—give up the very thing you're doing the business for. Here's an example. If you're in this biz so you can have more time with your family, initially, this will probably take you away from them even more in the beginning. Or maybe you're doing this business so you can have more time and money to travel. You may have to cut out the few trips you have planned now so that you can enjoy a lot more of them later.

If you're one of those people we talked about earlier who's not good with delayed gratification, this won't be easy. This is probably the biggest reason so many people quit before they reap the rewards of their efforts. Just be prepared for this to be one of the most challenging hurdles you'll face. But for those who make the sacrifices, the payoff is more than worth it. You'll earn back the

THIS BUSINESS IS
LIKE GOING
ON A DIET;
IT'S EASY UNTIL
YOU GET HUNGRY.

time and freedom tenfold. Speaking of time, just about everyone feels like they don't have enough time to do this business, but we all have the same 24 hours a day. If you have time to read this book, you have time to do this business. It's all about our choices.

THE FIRST YEAR IN THE LIFE OF A NMer

Some things about NM will seem pretty counterintuitive. It's best to learn about those things as soon as you get started, and that's yet another benefit of being coached by your sponsor and/or upline. Many people look at this business and decide to approach it in the same way they've approached life up until this point. We're taught to study, learn, and then we'll be prepared for the task. But NM is a business that is all about "on the job training." It's sort of like riding a bike; you've just got to experience it to get the hang of it. Once you do it; it becomes second nature. But in the same way as learning to ride a bicycle; reading an instruction manual about it won't ever be the same as actually doing it.

With a strong enough desire, a solid belief in what you're representing, and support from your sponsor or upline, you can begin immediately. Everyone's goals, skills, and situations are different. However, for most people—because of the tremendous level of support from your upline, a good system, and the ability to use "tools"—you can start right away. Getting into massive action is a very successful way to approach this business.

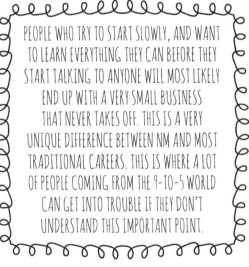

Think about an airplane taking off the runway. Will the plane take off the ground if the pilot only uses 25% of the power? 50%? 75%? No, the plane needs 100% full throttle all at once to lift off the ground. The difference between using 25% or even 75% means that the plane would never have the momentum needed to thrust it into the air. This business works exactly the same way.

One of the great things about this biz, though, is that momentum can happen the minute you're ready. Even if someone has been dabbling in their business for

PEOPLE WHO TRY TO START SLOWLY, AND WANT TO LEARN EVERYTHING THEY CAN BEFORE THEY START TALKING TO ANYONE WILL MOST LIKELY END UP WITH A VERY SMALL BUSINESS THAT NEVER TAKES OFF. THIS IS A VERY UNIQUE DIFFERENCE BETWEEN NM AND MOST TRADITIONAL CAREERS. THIS IS WHERE A LOT OF PEOPLE COMING FROM THE 9-TO-5 WORLD CAN GET INTO TROUBLE IF THEY DON'T UNDERSTAND THIS IMPORTANT POINT.

years, the moment they decide to do whatever it takes—and give it their full throttle—they can turn it around.

Momentum is necessary for a NM business to take off. When you first start your excitement is contagious. As soon as you find your first business partner, you start to see the power of leverage that this business provides. In the beginning you might even feel a little obsessed. Seize that energy and operate with a sense of urgency. When you're in this ideal place and things are starting to happen, people will listen to you and will become customers and/or business partners. It's so important to maximize that momentum. You'll probably feel a little overwhelmed when things take off. Just know that the first three months can be challenging, as you try to balance your life and grow your business. It requires faith. Trust that as long as you're doing what needs to be done, the rewards will come.

AFTER THE FIRST YEAR...

Once you've started to grow a team, the activity of your NM business will look different than it did in the very beginning. You'll be both building your own personal network, and coaching and mentoring the people you've sponsored. Your role is to help them become strong, self-sufficient leaders. Avoid getting "manager-itis" at this stage. Your purpose is to inspire others, not manage them. Another important lesson that you'll quickly learn is that not everyone who says they're serious will do what's necessary to be successful. You can't want this business more for someone than they want it themselves. Believe us that will happen. Reps who you've sponsored will quit. When they do, there will be people in their downline who will reach out to you for help. Support them the same way you'd support someone who you personally sponsored. Sometimes you'll be surprised. You'll discover a new leader on your team who you didn't even know before. That's one of the really cool things about this biz: leaders can emerge from any level of your business.

A "kick-butt NM leader":

- Inspires and coaches others to achieve their goals.
- Performs where others are too afraid to.
- Gets the job done, whether others choose to join in or not.
- Is committed to constant, honest self-evaluation and personal development.
- Sets and maintains the right example in all areas of their professional and personal life.
- Has an organizational game plan that involves the success of others.

AFTER 3-5 YEARS...

If your business has grown, and you have a huge team, your activity will vary depending on the strength of the leaders. If you have strong leaders, you won't be as directly involved with those teams. If you don't have strong leaders, you may still need to be involved in their downline. The strength of your business correlates directly with the caliber of your leadership team—that's why you always want to have the mindset to "sponsor up." That means you're always looking for people who are better than you are in some ways. If you have a leader who leaves, or needs to step back for a while due to some unexpected circumstances, you'll want to step back in and be the leader to those people on the team. You'll want to look for capable, determined people and support them in growing into a leadership role.

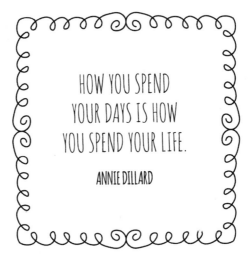

HOW YOU SPEND
YOUR DAYS IS HOW
YOU SPEND YOUR LIFE.

ANNIE DILLARD

CHAPTER THREE

IT'S TIME TO CHOOSE A NETWORK MARKETING COMPANY YOU'LL LOVE

Choose

CHooz *verb:* Pick out or select (someone or something) as being the best or most appropriate of two or more alternatives.

CHOOSING THE RIGHT COMPANY FOR YOU

So you're still here…which hopefully means you feel like you have what it takes to slip off those uncomfortable shoes and into some flip flops. Now we'll help you figure out what comes next: choosing a company that you'll love. In this chapter we'll break down the important stuff you'll need to know about how to tell if a company is legit, what it means to do proper due diligence, and how much is reasonable to invest when you're getting started.

CHOOSING A COMPANY: WHAT'S LOVE GOT TO DO WITH IT?

In case you haven't guessed it already, choosing a company can be a lot like choosing a spouse, because the company you choose will (fingers crossed) be a life-long partner. And while your chosen company won't be the big spoon on cold nights, it will be there with you in product development, legal and financial issues, customer service, product fulfillment, data processing, international expansion, public relations, and so much more. That's why it's super-duper important that you're proud of the company and its leaders. Are they on the same page as you when it comes to important things like ethics, values, goals and leadership? They should be, because all of those factors are critical to your success in NM.

Every Rep you speak to is going to tell you their company and their products are the best. That's a really, really good thing. That means they're enthusiastic about, and believe in, the NM Business in a Box they've chosen. Listen to them. Listen to what they're so excited about. Find out why they believe in the products and the company. Do these same things resonate with you? This is your business, so the way you feel about it is very important. You need to feel that same kind of excitement about your Business in a Box.

Most NM companies have a strong culture, meaning the behaviors and beliefs that are characteristic of the group. There are lots of NM companies to choose from, and they're all unique, so it's important to find one you love, believe in, and are totally proud of. The easiest way to feel out a NM company's vibe is to spend some time around the people within it. You can also tell a lot about a company's culture by the type of people it attracts, so it is definitely worth your while to attend a few functions and/or meet with some of the Reps. Once you find your perfect match, commit to sticking with them through thick and thin and you'll undoubtedly build that empire you've been dreaming of.

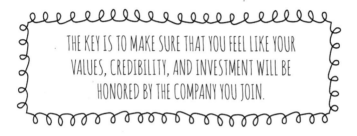

THE KEY IS TO MAKE SURE THAT YOU FEEL LIKE YOUR VALUES, CREDIBILITY, AND INVESTMENT WILL BE HONORED BY THE COMPANY YOU JOIN.

VETTING A NM COMPANY'S LEGITIMACY

In the United States, NM has been a legitimate, legal model to pay independent Reps to sell products for more than 50 years. During that time, NM has repeatedly been upheld by the federal and state courts as a legal distribution and compensation method when the following guidelines are being followed:

1. The main objective of the business is selling viable products or services at a reasonable price. Meaning, the focus of the company is to sell real products or services that people actually want to buy and/or have use for, and can do so affordably.

2. Each independent Rep maintains a retail/preferred client customer base, usually with at least ten or more people, who are just buying products on a regular basis, resulting in a

business with more customers than Reps, not the other way around.

3. Potential incomes for recruiting others are not promised; or in some states, even mentioned.

AGAIN...THE PRIORITY HAS TO BE SELLING PRODUCT, NOT SELLING PEOPLE.

4. Representatives are not paid any type of head hunting fee or bonus for the mere act of recruiting others i.e., Reps are not being paid to recruit new people, but are paid to share the products with other peeps.

5. Reps are not encouraged to buy more product than they can reasonably use and/or resell within 30 days. Meaning, don't stock your garage full of products…that's where your car belongs.

6. The company must refund unsold product and sales materials—including enrollment fees—if a Rep chooses to resign. Think of this as a money back guarantee of sorts. If you decide this biz isn't your bag, you won't be stuck with a bunch of products and brochures you can't use. Because that's seriously un-cool. It's always a good idea to check out the company's product return policy before you join. Make sure you know if there's a time limit on returning products.

The earning potential that NM offers is huge for both network marketers and the companies using this distribution method. So naturally, it has and will continue to attract some very "dynamic" promoters – some are ethical, some not. The truth is, like with most good things, there are people out there who will try to take advantage of the situation. Unfortunately, there have been more than a few NM companies that have crossed the line legally, and have ended up being the subject of negative media, as well as civil and criminal penalties. Which is why it's so important to remember that this is a major business decision. **DO YOUR DUE DILIGENCE!**

DUE DILIGENCE FOR NEWER NM COMPANIES

There are good, bad, and indifferent butchers, bakers, and candlestick makers. The same is true about doctors, lawyers, accountants... and NM companies. Building a business is hard enough without having to worry about the company's stability or ethics. Knowing how to pick the right company is crazy important, you've gotten that much, but how do you actually do it?

For starters, it's important to ask questions and lots of them. You want to make sure a company has demonstrated that

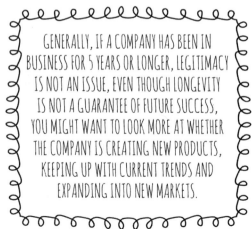

GENERALLY, IF A COMPANY HAS BEEN IN BUSINESS FOR 5 YEARS OR LONGER, LEGITIMACY IS NOT AN ISSUE, EVEN THOUGH LONGEVITY IS NOT A GUARANTEE OF FUTURE SUCCESS, YOU MIGHT WANT TO LOOK MORE AT WHETHER THE COMPANY IS CREATING NEW PRODUCTS, KEEPING UP WITH CURRENT TRENDS AND EXPANDING INTO NEW MARKETS.

they have a sustainable business, meaning they aren't selling something no one actually wants, or that could be totally unnecessary in a few years. Make sure they are growing ethically, that they're not cheating the system or, even worse, trying to cheat you! And lastly, check to make sure they honor their Reps and customers, because Reps and customers are the peanut butter and jelly of every NM company, and doing right by the peeps that are buying and selling their products or services is part of what keeps a good NM company around for the long haul.

HERE ARE SOME TIPS ON THINGS TO CONSIDER (ESPECIALLY WITH A NEWER COMPANY):

- Check out the state/province corporate registry (if possible) to confirm the company is legally registered. Then search the trademark database and their website to make sure they all point to the same entity or address. If they don't, it's not necessarily a bad thing, but at least one of these should point to the company's headquarters.
- Ask questions about financial stability. What is their backing? Are they debt free?
- What is the experience of the management team?
- What are the company's goals for expanding internationally? Expanding internationally too aggressively can create challenges.
- Some companies actually allow you to sell and/or legally will

(i.e., pass along to your heirs) your business and network of customers you've built. If this is important to you, does the company you're considering allow this?

- Beware of a company whose Reps promise quick money with little effort, and/or Reps who say you don't need to share, recommend, or sell the product or service. This is a huge red flag. ⟵
- Exercise caution around Reps who promise to do the selling for you, and companies that have a compensation plan that encourages you to "buy in" with a large order.
- Beware of a company that has frequent backorders, meaning they can't fulfill orders being taken. (Backorders happen, but shouldn't happen very often.)
- Beware of companies that are late with commission checks. Complete and timely payments are one sign of a healthy company, anything other than that might be a red flag.

ESTABLISHED OR START-UP: HOW DO YOU CHOOSE?

You may or may not have heard the term "ground floor opportunity," and you may or may not be wondering what that even means. For those scratching their heads, the term "ground floor opportunity" means a company and, in this case, the NM company is a start-up or is relatively new. There are peeps out there who will pose this as a highly valuable "opportunity" because the theory is that if you "get in early"; you'll have dibs on being one of the first to introduce these products to people. Thus there would be more people available to join *your business*; which would mean having more people in your downline than if you joined an older or more established company.

If you're trying to figure out just how important it really is to get in "on the ground floor" of a new company, you'll want to consider another perspective. Typically, getting in on the ground floor can also be one of the worst times to join. Here are a few reasons why:

- 85% of NM companies will fail within their first five years. It's just a fact.
- New companies are on a learning curve and may not be able to put its best foot forward early on.
- It can take years to develop competent, experienced staff, reliable procedures, and efficient services.

Not always, but in general, the best time to join a company is when that company is at least five years old. By year five, a company has a way higher chance of staying in business, has proven it's growing ethically, and that it takes good care of its Reps and customers.

If you are currently considering a new company, just make sure that you:

A. Have done your due diligence and asked the important questions listed above.
B. Believe in a product or service the company is offering.
C. Believe in the founders or the people running the company.

LET'S TALK ABOUT SATURATION

Saturation

sat·u·ra·tion / 'saCHə'rāSH(ə)n *noun:* The state or process that occurs when no more of something can be absorbed, combined with, or added.

If you're considering joining a new company and you're being told "You need to get in fast so that you'll have a chance to be at the top of the company," or "You'll be able to get in before the market becomes saturated," you're basically hearing a slightly different version of the "ground floor opportunity" theory. This type of recruiting method reeks of a very unprofessional approach to rush someone into signing up. If you've been following along, the benefit of growing a NM biz is that it will be around for the long haul. Pressuring someone about needing to get in quick makes no sense if your goal is to build a long-term network of happy product users, right? The assumption behind this tall tale is that when the market becomes saturated with a particular product, the demand will run out—i.e., when the market gets saturated with Reps, there will be a shortage of customers to go around. This theory holds no merit. The only way a market could ever become completely saturated is if every single man, woman, and child had already become a Rep or a customer, using a particular product. This idea is completely ludicrous. Not only has this never happened in NM, it's never happened anywhere, with anything, on this planet.

CHOOSING YOUR BUSINESS IN A BOX: NM VS. DIRECT SALES

You've got needs and you've got goals and it's important that you know the company you're choosing is on the same wavelength as you when it comes to achieving them. Making money is great, but not all earning po-

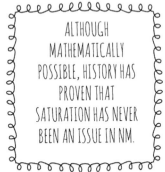

ALTHOUGH MATHEMATICALLY POSSIBLE, HISTORY HAS PROVEN THAT SATURATION HAS NEVER BEEN AN ISSUE IN NM.

tential is the same, as we've covered previously. So in order to set up realistic expectations about the money you're going to make, you need to make sure your financial goals are actually attainable with the company you're joining. You may want to take another peek at the chart on page 43 to determine whether a direct sales or a network marketing model will best meet your needs in the long and short term. But in case flipping pages is too much of a pain, let's do a quick recap of the differences between the two:

Direct Sales

Direct sales typically provides the opportunity to make money quickly (which we referred to earlier as "right now money"), based on your own personal sales. To do this type of business, it's important you love and believe in the products and the company you're representing. Your primary role will be on demonstrating the products and following up with excellent customer service.

Network Marketing

NW pays you for your personal sales, but also for building a team of Reps. If you're looking to build a long-term, residual income business, this is the model that will probably provide the best fit. To create lasting and ongoing income, you'll want to choose consumable products or services that need to be re-ordered on a regular basis. The focus of this business model involves representing both the products and the biz and building a network of consumers. You will also be responsible for sponsoring, teaching, and supporting other Reps in building their businesses. Enrolling, coaching, and leading others is very much a part of this model. Having good leadership skills or being willing to develop them is pretty important.

TO CONSUME OR NOT TO CONSUME... THAT IS THE QUESTION

You may still think of network marketing companies as just selling plastic containers, cookware, skin care, and make-up, but today's NM companies represent all kinds of things you probably are already

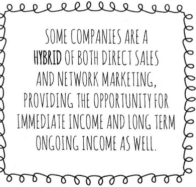

SOME COMPANIES ARE A **HYBRID** OF BOTH DIRECT SALES AND NETWORK MARKETING, PROVIDING THE OPPORTUNITY FOR IMMEDIATE INCOME AND LONG TERM ONGOING INCOME AS WELL.

buying somewhere else. Products range from personal care items you and your family use on a daily basis—like shampoo, deodorant, toothpaste, make-up, vitamins, and meals—to home accessories, air and water purifiers, gardening supplies, household cleaning items, candles, jewelry, clothing, cookware, legal aid, travel needs, and even your utilities, like phone services and home energy.

When considering which NM Business in a Box is right for you, there are a couple of things to consider about the products or service you represent. Products and services sold in NM fall into two very distinct categories: consumable and non-consumable.

"Consumables" as we refer to them in this biz, are products that consumers use on a day-to-day basis, products that get used up and need to be replenished. Consumable products can look like everything from health and fitness supplements and personal care products, to greeting cards and telecommunications.

Non-consumables, however, are one-time-sale items or things that don't need to be replaced as often, like cookware, home accessories, jewelry, clothing, and water purifiers.

The reason this distinction is important for you to know is that, typically, to create residual income, you want to find a product or service that is consumable and requires regular purchasing. Consumable products are especially important to the equation of building residual income through the model of "a lot of people, each doing a little

CHOOSING THE RIGHT BUSINESS IN BOX FOR YOU DEPENDS UPON YOUR GOALS, THE KIND OF ACTIVITY YOU WANT TO BE IN, AND ALIGNING YOURSELF WITH A COMPANY THAT WILL BEST HELP YOU REACH YOUR GOALS.

bit." Which means you're building a network of consumers, people who repeatedly use the products, versus the typical direct selling model of "one and done."

COMPENSATION IS HIGHEST FOR THE ACTIVITY THE COMPANY WANTS REPS TO PARTICIPATE IN, AND LESS FOR THE ACTIVITY THAT DOESN'T FIT THEIR BUSINESS MODEL.

DETERMINING WHAT KIND OF ACTIVITY THE COMPANY'S COMP PLAN REWARDS: A QUICK GUIDE TO COMP PLANS

We're going to level with you: compensation plans can be very complicated. And it doesn't help matters that every company has its own unique plan. But despite no two ever being exactly alike, they're all designed to encourage and reward the sale of products. The comp plan usually offers rewards for two types of activities: personal sales and team building. Eventually it's going to be important that you understand your company's plan well enough to help educate others, but it's definitely not life or death that you know it like the back of your hand before joining a company. And almost no one ever does. With that being said, here's the gist of what you need to know now…

THERE ARE THREE PRIMARY INCOME OPPORTUNITIES:

1. **Selling product** – "Right now money." You'll get the product at wholesale and sell the product at the suggested retail

price, which generates commissions from your own personal effort. This is called "direct sales."

Side note: many NM companies also offer the option of customers purchasing products at a "preferred client" discount, usually lower than retail but higher than a Rep would pay.

2. **Business Building** – "Long term compensation." This is where you recruit (or sponsor) other Reps and receive an override from what they sell or use, and who they sponsor. There are usually multiple levels of compensation in this type of earning, hence the term "multi-level marketing."

3. **Additional Income Opportunities** – "Extra income opportunities." Depending on the company you choose, there are usually other ways to earn income through bonuses, free products, trips, car bonuses, gifts, etc.

THE SKINNY ON COMP PLANS

The most common types of plans used by NM companies are: Binaries, Unilevels, Bilaterals, Trilaterals, Break-a-ways, or a hybrid of some of these.

We could give you definitions and examples but, honestly, it's hard to provide a good "Reader's Digest" version, so suffice it to say that you just need to know the basics and rely on your sponsor to help you along the way.

DIRECT SALES INCOME VS NM INCOME

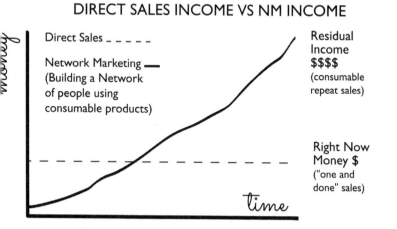

Just like the continuum chart of income from direct sales and NM you'll find a pretty wide range of philosophies when it comes to comp plans. Some reward sales to customers more than team building, and some reward team building more than sales to customers. Either way, they were all created with the same intention: to pay you on the sales of a multi-generational team. It's a good idea to look at the compensation plan as a way of understanding the philosophy of the company and what its priorities are, and make sure they match the way you'd like to build your business.

For comparison's sake, it may seem like a good idea to try and figure out all the comp plans before you decide to join a particular company, but that's not really necessary as long as you feel confident that there are people achieving success at each of the various levels in the company you're considering. The most important thing you need to figure out is whether you're most interested in earning immediate income and want to focus on selling the product to earn retail profits, or if your goal is to earn long-term, residual income by building a network of consumers and leading a team of Reps. Once you pinpoint your choice, you'll want to choose a company with a comp plan that pays you for doing that kind of activity. You can trust that reputable NM companies have pay plans that are designed to reward you, not cheat you. If the company you choose is attractive, exciting, growing, and has sales leaders who are successful, then you can pretty much trust that the plan must be working. We're not saying don't ask questions that are important to you. Just don't get too caught up in the details, at this point. As long as you stay connected to your sponsor or upline, you'll be able to learn the ropes as you go along.

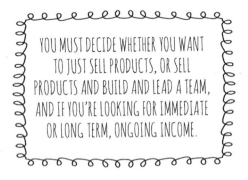

YOU MUST DECIDE WHETHER YOU WANT TO JUST SELL PRODUCTS, OR SELL PRODUCTS AND BUILD AND LEAD A TEAM, AND IF YOU'RE LOOKING FOR IMMEDIATE OR LONG TERM, ONGOING INCOME.

Here's a basic idea of how all plans pay out:

- Your personal sales. You may earn 20% to 35% in retail profits on your own customers.
- Your first generation (those you personally sponsored). You may earn 5-10% on their sales.
- Your second generation. You may earn 5-10% on their sales.
- Your third generation. You may earn 5-7% on their sales.
- Your fourth generation. 5-7%
- Fifth Generation. 5-7%
- Sixth. 3-5
- Seventh. 3-5%
- Eighth. 2-4%
- Ninth. 1-2%
- Tenth. 1%

So, as you can see, you're compensated less and earn a smaller percentage of the commission—also referred to as an override—the further removed the sales are from you. This is fair because you should have an increasingly higher number of Reps selling and leading their own teams at each generation, so your ongoing efforts are clearly much less. Your personal involvement in leadership and training have less and less to do with the actual sales the more removed you are from future generations.

Using the analogy of a family again as a great-great grandmother you wouldn't have as much hands-on effort with a new baby in your family as it's mother does. The baby is still part of your family, but you don't have the same responsibilities you did with your own child. As you sponsor Reps who become leaders, their new Reps will look to their upline and those who are closest to them for the greatest support.

In addition to these generational commissions, you can also qualify for a variety of leadership or team bonuses. When you add them all up (and to be clear, you won't earn all of these on all sales), the total payout from the company on any particular sales order will be 45%-50%. The company designs the plan so that it isn't paying out more than 50%. That's because anything more than fifty percent would eat into the expenses your company needs for producing the product, overhead, research and development, expansion, business development, taxes and profit, etc. As we've mentioned previously, most NM companies also offer lots of additional perks—like cars, vacations, jewelry, and other types of products—in addition to the cash bonuses.

THINGS YOU SHOULD KNOW ABOUT EARNING A NM PAYCHECK

While you definitely don't need to understand everything about a company's compensation plan before you get started, it is essential that you learn about any requirements the company has in place that could affect your ability to make the most of the compensation plan.

And here's what we mean by that: study each title and bonus *that currently applies to you* and *could* apply to you in the near future. Just make sure you're completely clear about what the requirements are to advance and earn bonuses *at your current level.* It's a smart idea to take it a step further and ask your sponsor or upline to continue to go over the parts of the plan that currently apply to you, at each new level, *as you get there.* Be sure that you're clear. Get all of your questions answered. Here's why: if the volume requirement to earn a bonus or promote is $5,000, you don't want to end the pay period with $4,999. $4,999 is not $5,000 and no one is going to bend the rules for you.

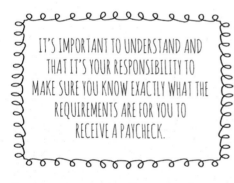

IT'S IMPORTANT TO UNDERSTAND AND THAT IT'S YOUR RESPONSIBILITY TO MAKE SURE YOU KNOW EXACTLY WHAT THE REQUIREMENTS ARE FOR YOU TO RECEIVE A PAYCHECK.

Okay, so now that you get how you can earn money in your NM biz, it's super important to look at any minimums that are required to get paid. Do you have to order or sell a certain amount of product every month? For most companies the answer is yes and the amount you need to buy or sell every month will vary from $100-$200. So you definitely want to make sure you feel good about using and/or selling that much, personally, every month. It's pretty common for people to look at this requirement as a business expense, but we encourage you to look at it for what it really is: you're buying products you love and want to use monthly. These are the products you'll recommend to others and on which you're going to earn a profit, so they're definitely not just another cost to add to your "budget." It's important for you to earnestly become "a product of the product" you're representing.

Now let's talk paychecks. Your NM paycheck can come from various types of activity. You'll be paid on the product/service sales you generate yourself plus an override or small percentage of the volume of the Reps you sponsor. You may want to look at how many Rep levels deep you get paid, especially if your company says you get paid to infinity. Let us explain what we mean by that. Again, using the family tree analogy, you want to know how many generations after you you're compensated for. Each of those sales can be traced back to you. If a company says it pays you to infinity that would mean that you would be paid a small percentage of every sale, in all of your future generations, forever, for your initial efforts. **Be sure to do your due diligence,** read over the compensation plan, and go over this with your sponsor or someone in your upline who is able to help you understand the compensation plan. But, if you get paid to at least five levels/generations deep, meaning someone who you sponsored has now sponsored someone, who has now sponsored someone, who has now sponsored someone, who has now sponsored someone (whew, got all that?)… then the plan is probably legit.

An income should never be from recruiting Reps only—that's considered a pyramid.

Some jurisdictions consider this to be a sign of a pyramid scheme and companies have been shut down, and owners arrested for these types of operations.

IF YOU'RE PAID A "BONUS" (ALSO CALLED A "TRAINING BONUS") FOR EACH REP YOU SPONSOR, CONSIDER THIS A GIANT RED FLAG FOR ILLEGAL ACTIVITY.

HI, MY TITLE IS...MY TITLE IS ...WHAT?

We wish NMers could learn to stop using all the jargon— it's like hearing someone speak a foreign language.

If you've ever had a conversation with a NMer, you've probably experienced this. You're having a normal conversation and then suddenly they start talking about being an Elite Diamond, Ruby, or Executive Triple Black Star. What the heck is up with that? The titles vary from sounding corporate-like to something straight out of a frat movie.

Every NM company and compensation plan has "titles" or pin levels. (They call them pin levels because in certain companies you'd receive a lapel pin for some of the titles. Retro, right?) The deal with these titles is simply to signify where you are in terms of your rank and earning level. With every advance in title comes higher or deeper commissions, leadership bonuses, pools and/or matching bonuses, and other perks. Once you start to sponsor others and build your team, you'll want to have a general idea and access to someone who knows about your company's levels/titles, what it takes to advance to the next title, and how the compensation differs at each. And if you are a NMer who uses these terms when talking to someone about your business, please stop. It's confusing and sounds a little bit like you have joined a cult. When you're talking to someone outside of your company, and introducing or referencing someone within your company who has achieved a certain level or title, it would be so much more enlightening to say something like, "There are four levels in our company, and this person has achieved the top level." Rather than saying, "She's a double extra elite ruby!" This lingo only makes sense to peeps that are in your own company.

LEGALITIES/JOINING MULTIPLE COMPANIES/CHANGING COMPANIES

So you've just drank the NM Kool-Aid and you're ready to jump in head first. There are so many great companies out there—how do you choose just one? Maybe you have friends or family members in different companies. Maybe you're thinking that doubling down will increase your odds of being able to make some serious moolah. Either way, you're not alone: there are always people who consider joining more than one company when they first start out. But the bummer news is that most companies just aren't having that. So, generally, it's not recommended to be in more than one company at a time. And let's get real; the energy you're going to need to build one business is enough without adding the complexity of attempting to build more than one business at the same time, especially if you're looking at building a network marketing team. Maybe with direct sales, you can find complimentary products to represent, but make sure it's not a no-no with your company first. If your goal is to create a hefty stream of income and build an awesome NM business, we suggest funneling all of your mojo in one direction.

BUILDING TWO NM BUSINESSES WOULD BE KIND OF LIKE HAVING TWO SPOUSES. IT'S NOT RECOMMENDED!

HOW MUCH DOES IT COST TO START A BUSINESS IN A BOX?: THE 3-MINUTE GUIDE TO INVESTING IN YOUR BUSINESS

In the immortal words of Puff Daddy, "It's all about the Benjamins, baby." That's because whether you have a little or a lot, being cautious with your hard earned dough is numero uno. When you're considering joining a NM company, it's a smart idea to make sure the sign up and initial purchase costs the company requires you to make are a good fit for you and your wallet.

For some reason, people joining a direct sales/NM company always seem to be looking at how little they can invest, how little work they

BUT YOUR NM BIZ ISN'T LIKE BUYING A HOUSE TO FLIP; IT'S MORE LIKE FINDING A SPOUSE. IF YOU APPLIED THE SAME THOUGHT PROCESS TO DATING AS YOU DID TO HOUSE FLIPPING, IT'S PRETTY MUCH GUARANTEED THAT YOU'D END UP UNHAPPY OR ALONE.

can do, and how much money they can earn. Now, we can see how this may seem like the smart approach if you were, let's say…flipping a house. If that were the case, you'd definitely want to try to get the most bang for the least amount of effort and buck. What great love story ever started with someone saying "I want to find my soul mate and I want to do it with as little effort and money as possible"? Prince Charming wouldn't have been much of a charmer, would he?

The moral of the story is that this is a business endeavor and if you treat this like a real business, you'll be paid accordingly. If you treat this as if it's a hobby, you will be paid like it's a hobby. And hello! Compared to any other type of business, the amount of money it takes to get started is super low; combine that with the potential to earn a very high return and it should be a no-brainer.

Now let's talk about enrollment fees. These typically range from $0 to $500. We find the norm is about $100. This could include a variety of things, such as catalogues, forms, possibly a few videos, and maybe a little bit of product or samples. While $100 may not get you set up for business, it will typically get your registered as a Rep and that's the first important step. Beyond getting registered— whether that's free or $100—you'll want to learn as much as you can about the product line and the system that's used for selling it and for building a team. This will help you decide how much and where else to invest in your business.

ORDER #1...WHAT SHOULD I BUY?

This is probably going to be the most exciting order you make, but before you go all *Supermarket Sweep* or get freaked out about having to buy a ton of product, let's talk this through. If you're going to host parties or do sales events, you're usually better off having product on-hand to show, tell, and sell. That's usually better than simply relying on a catalog or website to get the job done. Think about it: why does everyone love going to Costco so much? One word: samples. People are way more inclined to buy stuff when they can actually try it out first. With this type of business model, it's not crazy for you to consider purchasing $500-$1,000 in products and marketing materials. It's hard to justify why you would ever need more than that, unless it's for your own personal use, given you can reorder and replenish your supply anytime and have it within 5-10 days.

Bottom line: determine what works best for you. Let's say that rather than having products on-hand to demo and sell, you'd prefer to be a product of the products yourself. You want to use them yourself, share what you love about them, and then show others how to do the same. You can do that! And if there are a gazillion different products in your company, and you aren't able to try them all when you're first starting out, ask for testimonials from your sponsor and/or your upline. With testimonials from real, live people, you'll be able to share stories about the products and the results people have had with them.

In this model, you don't have to inventory and deliver the product, or even collect the money because your company does all the dirty work for you. Your peeps simply purchase the products they want online via your introduction, and the products will be sent directly from the company. Think of it like a virtual business where your website is the store and you're the cheerleader for the products. So simple. You're probably already doing that now without being paid for it.

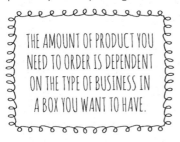

THE AMOUNT OF PRODUCT YOU NEED TO ORDER IS DEPENDENT ON THE TYPE OF BUSINESS IN A BOX YOU WANT TO HAVE.

Beware of any sponsor, upline, or company that encourages you to buy more product than you clearly need for immediate sales, events, or to be used as a business tool. Unfortunately, it's a pretty common practice to encourage a new Rep to buy whatever sales volume is required to advance to a certain title. This type of situation might sound something like, "Starting at this position shows you're serious and puts you in a position to earn higher bonuses right away…"

This may make sense in some cases, but it's definitely not the right option for everyone. A lot depends upon the new Rep's budget, goals, circle of influence, and personal circumstances. It's the responsibility of a sponsor to consider each situation individually and always put the best interests of the new Rep first when helping them place their first order. As you now know, your sponsor is going to earn a commission on your initial purchase, so make sure the logic of what you're purchasing is in line with how you intend to build your biz. Buying a bunch of products and having them just sit there staring at you won't get you very far. Ultimately, the only way to grow your business is for you to talk about and/or share the products with others.

Regardless of *how* you decide to run your Business in a Box, it's important to understand what your costs will be up front. The great news is that your sponsor or upline should be able to talk you through the costs and expenses and give you lots of tips and advice along the way.

FOR NOW, HERE ARE A FEW QUESTIONS TO ASK:

- Is it required that I purchase a certain amount of product to demonstrate?
- Does the company have tools and resources for me?
- Do they provide samples, and are they samples that I would be likely to use?

BUYER'S REMORSE HAPPENS. WHAT ABOUT RETURNS?

It's a pretty good idea to find out about a company's return pol-

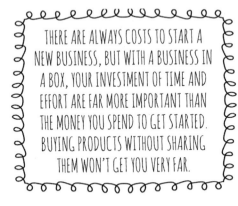

THERE ARE ALWAYS COSTS TO START A NEW BUSINESS, BUT WITH A BUSINESS IN A BOX, YOUR INVESTMENT OF TIME AND EFFORT ARE FAR MORE IMPORTANT THAN THE MONEY YOU SPEND TO GET STARTED. BUYING PRODUCTS WITHOUT SHARING THEM WON'T GET YOU VERY FAR.

icies. If a customer or someone you've sponsored returns their products or cancels their membership, the company will usually deduct the commissions you previously earned from your next commission check. This is why it's very important to educate new Reps about all of their options, before they place their initial order so they can make the right choice for *their* personal situation.

WEBSITES, MARKETING MATERIALS, TRAINING...OH MY!

Websites: some companies charge small fees for things like your own website/e-commerce site and renewal fees. Other companies may seem more Rep-friendly because they don't charge these fees. Keep in mind that nothing in

WHAT PRODUCTS TO BUY, AND HOW MUCH TO INITIALLY SPEND IS DEPENDENT ON THE GOALS AND RESOURCES

the world is free and even the so-called free stuff comes with a price. Remember that free haircut your friend got in college? So even if a company isn't charging you for these things specifically, it's a guarantee that these costs are built into their business plan somewhere. It might show up in higher product costs or lower commissions.

Training: even though these are usually pretty small expenses, you'll want to be prepared to invest in your education. There is no greater leverage, no greater ROI (Return on Investment), than investing in your own skills. Mad skills = mega confidence. Yeah, yeah, you may have paid your 100 bucks to join a company, but events are where the culture and spirit of your company seep in! There's no better way to get a true sense of how many people are in NM—and the level of profession-alism of the Reps in your company—than to attend a big conference. It's not unusual to have meetings with 10,000 or more people at these types of events. It's a great way to experience the vibe of your tribe. Your company will more than likely offer local, regional, and national events; the more events you attend, the stronger your skills and belief in your products and company will be. And remember your own belief is what will take you right to the top.

BEFORE YOU WRITE THAT CHECK, CONSIDER THIS:

- Does the company have the infrastructure to build your business the way you would like it built? Meaning if you're building a network of shoppers, do they have a website that is user friendly and allows your customers to easily shop for themselves?
- Does the company provide a personal website as part of the

enrollment fee, and if not, do they make one available for an affordable cost?

- Does the company have marketing and/or training materials that will support you in reaching your goals?
- How's the company's customer service? Do they offer a satisfaction guaranteed, money back return?

IN SUMMARY: 6 QUESTIONS TO ASK YOURSELF TO HELP YOU DECIDE ON A COMPANY

We make lots of decisions without giving them a lot of thought (remember acid wash jeans?), but choosing your perfect NM company shouldn't be one of those times. Deciding to buy a brand new ride is a big first step, but it's just that—a first step. Next you have to decide which one is coming home with you.

These 6 questions will help narrow down your options, vet your company of choice or, at the very least, shine a little light on the process.

1. *How much does it cost to register as a new Rep and what do you receive for your initial fee?*
   You will find a full range of options here from zero (free) to $500, but we've found the norm is usually under $100. What you'll receive will vary but might include some catalogues,

forms, videos, and maybe a little bit of product or samples to use. Let's keep it real though, 100 bones does not a business make, but it can get you registered as a Rep.

2. *What is the system for selling and building a team?*
    Beyond getting registered—whether that is free or $100—you'll want to learn as much as you can about the product line, your particular company's system for selling it, and for building a team, in order to decide how much and where to invest in your business.

3. *Is there a minimum monthly monetary requirement to earn a paycheck?*
    As we've said before, completely understanding the comp plan of a company is just not practical or necessary for most of us before we join a company. Once you get started, you'll want to understand the general requirements of what you're working towards, or at least make sure someone in your up-line is there to help you understand what you're aiming for. Your sponsor or upline should be able to answer the basic questions you have. There are usually monthly monetary requirements that you must fulfill. Remember, it's important to make note of the fact that if the require-ment is $150, $149 is not $150, so being close won't cut it. Some good questions to ask are: is there

COMPANIES AREN'T GOING TO MAKE EXCEPTIONS BECAUSE YOU DIDN'T UNDERSTAND THE RULES.

a minimum monthly purchase requirement? Is the monthly purchase requirement a reasonable amount for the products I'll need to replenish?

4. *What other expenses will be required?*
    Talking money can be a bummer unless it's about how much someone is going to give you. Knowing what financial expenses come with your new Business in a Box is not a bummer. Having this info is going to be vital to your success both long term and short term.

5. *Does the company culture match your needs?*
    Only you can decide if a company is your perfect match but keep in mind there is a tribe for every vibe.

6. *Does the company encourage direct sales activity, network marketing activity, or both?* (See chart on page 56)
    This question will directly influence your immediate and/or long-term income potential. Doing your homework in this department will ensure that the business model matches your needs and expectations now and in the long run.

WHEN SOMEONE SHARES
SOMETHING OF VALUE WITH YOU
AND YOU BENEFIT FROM IT,
YOU HAVE A MORAL
OBLIGATION TO SHARE IT.

CHINESE PROVERB

CHAPTER FOUR

IT'S TIME TO CHOOSE PRODUCTS YOU'RE EXCITED ABOUT

Product

prod·uct /ˈprädəkt/ *noun*: an article or substance that is manufactured or refined for sale.

HOW TO PICK PRODUCTS YOU LOVE AND THAT WILL LOVE YOU BACK

If you were ever an eight-year-old kid with a lemonade stand, you know firsthand how important it is to have a product high in demand. Just imagine if you had tried to launch your hot cocoa biz that summer instead of a lemonade stand! It's not a stretch to assume that you might have been a little disappointed. Those childhood lessons are still relevant now: choosing the right product to promote and sell is a very important step when deciding which Business in a Box to choose.

Have no fear; *The Guide* is here to help! Whether you've already found your perfect product of choice—or you're still on the hunt for the right one—this chapter covers what's important to look for in products or services, how many products are the right amount to represent, and other handy stuff to aid in your decision.

BIG DEAL OR NO BIG DEAL: PRODUCTS

Make no bones about it, the products or services a NM company offers ultimately determines the long-term success of its Reps. What that means for you is, if a company has quality, relevant products at a reasonable price, you're going to be a-okay in the long run. If they don't…well, you get the point. But that's only half the enchilada, because what also really, really matters is your confidence and unwavering belief in the products.

Think about it like this: you've found a new restaurant, nail polish, energy drink, whatever, and you're literally losing your mind over how well it works. Don't you want to share it with everyone around you? Why? Because it's just *that* good. "Hey, lady next to me in line at Starbucks…you look tired, have you ever tried an energy drink instead of coffee?" It's not just you, we promise. Most of us want to spread the word when we find a new, awesome something, and that's exactly what it takes to build your NM business.

We've talked a lot about the importance of your belief in the profession of NM, the business model, *and* the company…but what happens if the only thing that sounds like fun to you is selling the products?

YOUR BELIEF IN THE PRODUCTS IS ABSOLUTELY NECESSARY.

Good news! You can still build a strong direct sales business. A Rep headed on this route will probably want to focus their efforts on sharing the products, personally create a database of shoppers/customers, and get paid a thank you check for selling them to others.

The fact is that some people are just more comfortable representing the products, and have zero desire to sponsor, train, and lead others. You can choose to promote the products you love and get on with the business of making money, honey. Ain't this biz grand?

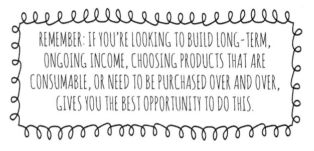

REMEMBER: IF YOU'RE LOOKING TO BUILD LONG-TERM, ONGOING INCOME, CHOOSING PRODUCTS THAT ARE CONSUMABLE, OR NEED TO BE PURCHASED OVER AND OVER, GIVES YOU THE BEST OPPORTUNITY TO DO THIS.

For residual income, think consumables: nutritional supplements, skin care, household cleaning products, telecommunications and energy.

PRODUCTS! SERVICES! WHAT ARE MY OPTIONS?

NM companies are a lot like shoes: they come in all different sizes and colors. There's no right or wrong shoe; there are just shoes that are right for you. And much like shoes, the numbers of product and service options you have when choosing a NM company are almost limitless. Love eating healthy? There's a NM product for you! Love learning stuff? There's a NM company for you! Addicted to the latest ways to stay youthful? There's also a NM company for you! Follow your passion and you'll probably find the perfect fit. Just in case, though, if you're still not sure where to start, here's a list of just some of the styles…uhh, options:

Nutrition. Skin Care. Technology. Vitamins. Essential Oils. Legal services. Internet malls. Toys. Food. Educational and motivational materials. Make-up and cosmetics. Water filters. Air filters. Books. Telecommunications. Energy. Diet and weight loss products. Anti-aging products. Household cleaning products. Scrapbooks. Greeting cards. Jewelry. Clothing. Personal care items. And even financial and travel services.

Getting excited? Us too! And that's just the tip of the iceberg, because at the rate this profession is growing, the range of products and services are sure to expand with it! If you're ready to explore your choices, and you don't know anyone personally to talk to, a good place to visit to find out more about the various options is: www.DSA. org. (Direct Selling Association— the association which we mentioned earlier—that most major network marketing companies belong to.)

THINGS TO CONSIDER AND ASK YOURSELF ABOUT TRENDS AND YOUR POTENTIAL AUDIENCE:

- Health and wellness, anti-aging, and longevity products are a huge trend and offer a wide audience of potential customers.
- Are the products in line with market trends?

- Are the products unique in some way from what is currently available in retail stores?
- Do the products have an obvious target market and mass appeal?

IS IT BEST TO CHOOSE A COMPANY THAT OFFERS ONE PRODUCT, A FEW, OR A LOT?

One product? Two products? Ten products? It can be really hard for some peeps to choose. Just like the type of car we drive, clothes we wear, and food we eat, at the end of the day it's totally a personal choice. There are a few pros and cons of selling a single product, or just a few products versus representing a whole boat load of different products. Let's break it down to help figure out where you stand. And, remember, this is all about considering what feels like the best *fit* for you. There are no wrong answers.

1. Who is the "target audience"?
2. Is there a particular demographic the product is attractive to?
3. If so, is this an audience you feel very comfortable with?
4. If the targeted audience is narrow, do you still feel confident there is enough demand from enough consumers to make the business viable long term?
5. If a company offers multiple products, do you feel over-whelmed by that, or do you feel more confident having the ability to represent more options for people?

6. How does the product stand up to trends? Is it something that is and will continue to be in demand?

7. Does the company plan to continue to add new products?

A BASIC GUIDE TO VETTING PRODUCTS

Let's face it: there are lots of times when we don't care if something is legit…like food court Chinese food and reality TV shows. But there are equally as many things that we do care about being legitimate, like plumbers and surgeons. NM products fall into the "do care" category, which is why we've created this handy list of things to consider:

- *Are the products patented and exclusive to the company?*
- *Are there competitive (meaning: similar) products out there?* If there are, you'll definitely want to learn the difference between those products and the ones your NM company provides. Psst! This could mean everything from pricing to ingredients!
- We know you're going to anyway…so, go ahead, give them a Google…but remember it may not be pretty! Consider the source when doing your research. If you end up confused, talk to a few Reps about why they chose a particular company. What do people who've used the products say about them?
- *Look at any claims that are being made about the efficacy of the products. Decide whether or not you would feel confident representing them.*

Are people blasting the product for some reason, or are there lots and lots of people singing its praises? You want to feel good about the products you're promoting, and their reputation in the marketplace is an important part of that. What is your own experience with them?

- *Do you see a need for the products? Are they in demand?*
Ever heard the expression "She could sell ice to an Eskimo?" Sure, okay, you may be a good salesperson, but why are you making life harder for yourself? Why not sell them a blanket! Or some firewood! Don't be that person. Choose a product you believe people actually want and need, and save yourself the headache.

- *Are you excited to use the products yourself and share them with others?*
Remember the lady in line at Starbucks that you couldn't wait to tell about your energy drink? You want to be fired up about your products! Authentic passion is contagious; if you're feeling it, everyone around you will, too.

- *Are the products something you would buy forever, regardless of whether you were a Rep or not?*
Talk about real-deal belief! This pretty much says it all… you're choosing a company for the long haul and the products that come with it. It's best to make sure you can really grow old together.

- *Do you believe the products will create loyal customers because of their benefits?*

  So you love them, but do you believe that other people will love them just as much as you, for no other reason than the fact that they're just plain great? Not that they should or will, but could the benefits of your products literally do the selling for you? If your answer is yes, congrats, you've found yourself a winner.

- *Are the products something you can recommend without reservation?*

  If you like the products, *but…* You haven't found your match, yet. Any reservations you have about your product will

FIND A PRODUCT YOU CAN GO "ALL IN" WITH OR KEEP SEARCHING.

  always be felt by the people you're recommending them to. That can't even be a notion in your noggin. And for the record, why would you want to recommend something you have reservations about anyway? Especially when there are so many companies to choose from!

- *Would your product sell without the business opportunity attached?*

  This is super important for a couple of reasons. Legitimate network marketing companies offer products/services people want to buy because they value them. When you represent a great product or service, you'll have lots of happy customers in your network—people who couldn't care

REMEMBER, IF A COMPANY IS ONLY ABOUT RECRUITING NEW REPS, THIS IS A BIG FAT RED FLAG.

less about the business but just want to use what you're offering. The opportunity to create an ongoing income by building a team of Reps is the icing on the cake!

Here's the skinny: if, in any way, you have to try to feel confident about the products, let this business opportunity go. It just won't work for you long term.

HOW IMPORTANT IS IT THAT I BE KNOWLEDGEABLE ABOUT THE PRODUCTS I CHOOSE TO REPRESENT?

CAN A GUY REPRESENT A COMPANY THAT SELLS MOSTLY TO WOMEN?

This is an important question to find the answer to as you are considering which products to represent. Does the company offer training about the products? If so, what kind and how is it delivered? Does the company provide resources like product sheets, videos, or links to information? How do you feel about the resources that are available? Does the company provide samples? Are the business tools reasonably priced?

There are Reps who feel they need to know every detail about each product/service they represent before they can talk to anyone.

There are others who couldn't care less about details. They just want to share their experiences with the products and why they love them. This has a lot to do with the type of person you are. Do you feel like your style is a good fit with the company culture that you're joining? Is everyone else pretty scientific and research focused? If so, and you're still feelin' like this is the one for you, are there resources about the product available? Or do you feel like you need a science degree to fit into the company culture?

Some people wonder how a man could sell products that mostly women use, and that brings up a topic that we'd be remiss to not touch upon. The most important thing about choosing the product you'll represent is that you feel excited about sharing it. That doesn't always have to mean you personally use the product, as long as your belief in the product is rock solid. Here's what we mean by that. The founder of Victoria's Secret was a man. He doesn't use their products (as far as we know…ha ha) but he saw a need, and grew a business out of fulfilling that need. If you believe there's a huge market for a product that a NM company fills, and you're excited and enthusiastic about representing the products, that's what's most important. Maybe you believe in the product's unique ingredients. Or the incredible results people are experiencing. Perhaps you see a cutting edge business opportunity, and you want to be a part of it.

It's all about your belief and *excitement* about the integrity of your products, and the solution they're providing to people who use them.

Bottom line: in this business, it's about authentically sharing

something you've found that you believe in. Your excitement and passion matter a lot. Your own belief and excitement are what people will hear, so just make sure you have that.

It's also important to remember: **facts tell, stories sell.** There are a lot of people who are highly educated, know all of the details, facts, and reasons why someone should want the products or service. But if they aren't enthusiastic and cannot convey belief; all of their knowledge may not get them very far. There's a saying in NM: ignorance on fire is better than knowledge on ice. Meaning it's not *necessary* to know everything there is to know about the products or service before you get started. Your sponsor can help you with that part. Knowing every detail and then keeping it "on ice" because you don't share it won't work. But if your style is that you need to do your homework first, do that. Just don't keep your knowledge to yourself. You could develop frostbite. You need to do what works for you. Just be honest with yourself. NM is all about sharing what you know with others. Ultimately, you've got be comfortable with doing that.

LET'S TALK INVENTORY: HOW MUCH DO I NEED?

As we've already said, the days of needing to have lots of products on hand are over. For most NM Reps, you'll need very little inventory. The preferred method—in all but a few circumstances (some party plans, etc.)—is having the products shipped directly from the company to the consumer.

That being said, those whose business is more direct sales focused, will usually need to have more products on hand, to provide better customer service to customers. If you're in a hybrid company, using both the direct sales and NM models of building your business, and you have customers in your network who call you for products, you may want to keep certain things on hand. In direct sales, the Reps usually like to deliver products to their customers, as another way to build the relationship, demonstrate the product, and perhaps sell their customers other items.

It's important as you consider the products you'll represent to make sure you're comfortable with the culture of the company, and the way they prefer their Reps conduct business. This is an important discussion to have with your sponsor. Ask her how much product she keeps on hand, and why? Can you see yourself doing what she does? Speaking of your sponsor…

JUST HOW IMPORTANT IS MY SPONSOR?

We've briefly mentioned a sponsor earlier, but this is a good time to explain more about their role in your NM business. Your sponsor is the person who brings you into a NM company and will mentor you. Think of your sponsor as your NM mom. She's your "go to" for any and all info you may need while you're learning the ropes. Anyone above her is part of your upline, sort of like your NM family.

So it looks like this:

Ideally, your sponsor will be someone who is positive, successful and committed to helping you succeed. Sponsors are a lot like a business partner and, like a business partner; your sponsor wants to help you succeed because they're also successful if *you're* successful. Remember all that  stuff about *residual* income? Well this is where it comes to life. Sponsoring is how you build residual income, and the better at it you are, the more successful you *all* become. So listen to what your sponsor and upline have to say. Be coachable, learn as much as you can from them, and hopefully, you'll want to follow their lead.

IMPORTANT NOTE: YOUR SPONSOR IS NOT RESPONSIBLE FOR YOUR SUCCESS. YOU AND YOU ALONE ARE RESPONSIBLE FOR YOUR SUCCESS. YOUR SPONSOR CAN HELP YOU, TRAIN YOU AND SUPPORT YOU, BUT NO ONE CAN DO IT FOR YOU. REMEMBER, YOU DIDN'T WIN THE LOTTERY; THIS IS A REAL BUSINESS SO IT'S IMPORTANT THAT YOU TREAT IT LIKE ONE!

When you sponsor a Rep, they become part of your downline, and you'll have your own family tree. When they share the products and business, and their friends become Reps and/or customers, they are also part of your downline, and it continues from there to include anyone who they sponsor. You're paid on your downline's "volume."

Okay, so what if you and your sponsor don't have a good working relationship? It happens; don't sweat it. Your best bet is to go to your sponsor's sponsor, and continue going up the line until you find someone who has the info you need. Whether it's about the compensation plan, products, or "how" to do

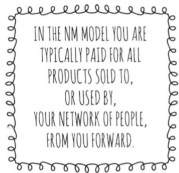

IN THE NM MODEL YOU ARE TYPICALLY PAID FOR ALL PRODUCTS SOLD TO, OR USED BY, YOUR NETWORK OF PEOPLE, FROM YOU FORWARD.

this business, you're going to have questions, so make sure to lean on your upline—that's what they're there for! The most important take away here is simply to make sure you have access to someone who understands what's required to be successful.

What if your direct sponsor is just getting started, too? The sweet thing about NM is that everyone starts at the same place, so that means even the person making a million dollars a year, at one point in time, was a newbie who just sponsored their first person. All that means is that if you and your sponsor start at the same time, and are both new, you can be mentored and learn the business together. Think of them as a workout buddy! This situation is also a bonus if you have someone with different strengths than you that you want to bring into your business right away.

So what does that mean? Let's say you love talking about your products—you could do it in your sleep—but you're not so great when it comes to explaining the business side of things. If you know someone who'd be a natural at presenting the business, but might not be as comfortable when it comes to sharing the products, it would be smart for the two of you to piggyback on each other's strengths. This business can be even more fun when you're learning and doing things with someone you really enjoy working with. So don't be afraid to grab a few friends and start growing your business together right away!

SOME QUESTIONS TO ASK YOUR SPONSOR, AND YOURSELF:

es her
.eason
.sonate
ith me?

1. What do you like most about the products and the company?

does this make sense to me?

2. What's your experience with people using the products? Who are competitors? What are the biggest challenges you've encountered? How do you respond to these things?

3. Will you show me how you share/present the products? How do you share the business? Will you do this for me until I learn how to do it myself?

can I see myself doing this?

4. What resources are available for me to plug into?

am I comfortable with the quality of the resources?

does this fit with what I envision for my business?

5.   What hours will you be available to help me?

6.   What kinds of events are offered locally? Out of state? How do you use these events to build your business?

does this sound reasonable to me?

7.   If I started today, what would I be doing and how would you be helping me?

am I excited to get started?

am I comfortable with these policies as a fit for the way I want to grow my business.

8.   If I'm thinking I'd like to market a certain way using the Internet-does the company have any restrictions about what can be done? Is anyone else in the company doing this? Can you show me some examples?

9.   Will I be able to access others in your upline if I need to?

if I need something that my sponsor can't provide, what other resources are available to me?

SPONSORING SOMEONE: IMPORTANT THINGS TO CONSIDER

When it comes to sponsoring family members and close friends—especially if they are signing up at the same time—it's important to take some time to really think about how you'll sign them up, and who will sponsor whom. If you don't feel like you have enough know-how to do this alone, ask for help from someone in your upline who really understands why this is so important. This may not seem like a big deal right now but believe us—it can be down the road. A NM business can turn into a sizable income steam, and we're paid on everyone who's in our downline, so deciding who will be in whose downline is an important decision. We don't mean to scare you, but when the time comes, be sure you're making an informed decision **before** you start signing people up. There are many variables to this situation depending on the company's compensation plan, so it's difficult to use more specific examples, but you'll be fine as long as you talk to someone in your upline who understands your company's comp plan.

SPONSORING/ PLACEMENT DECISIONS ARE IMPORTANT. THINK OF IT LIKE THE BUSINESS EQUIVALENT OF DOING A CROSSWORD PUZZLE IN PEN!

Does she sign up her mom first, then, sister one, direct to her mom, and then sister two, direct to sister one? How will sister two feel about this? What if sister two is the most serious about the biz….how do you know what to do? It's also very important that you're comfortable with your sponsor, because once you've signed up, most companies won't let you switch. If you find yourself in a situation where you truly feel like you and your sponsor are just not a good fit, it's usually a good idea to take some time to get real with yourself about why. Is your sponsor really the cause of your challenges, or is there something you need to change about yourself? There can be a tendency in this business to want to blame or resent your upline, whether it's because you're comparing them to someone else in the company, or you're just not getting the results you thought you would. Either way, here is the cold, hard truth:

DOGS "MARK THEIR TERRITORY" ... PEOPLE SHOULDN'T! (SORRY TO BE GROSS, BUT THIS IS A REAL PROBLEM.)

YOU DON'T NEED AN UPLINE TO BE SUCCESSFUL...YOU NEED A DOWNLINE. WHILE IT'S DEFINITELY NICE— AND A WHOLE LOT EASIER—TO HAVE THE SUPPORT AND GUIDANCE OF YOUR SPONSOR, ULTIMATELY, IF YOU REALLY WANT TO SUCCEED IN THIS BUSINESS, YOU'LL MAKE IT HAPPEN WITH OR WITHOUT ONE.

Determining who has the "right" to sponsor someone can be a *touchy* aspect of this biz. Sometimes a Rep will have handed out a sample, or spoken to someone they've met about their company, and then down the road this person gets to know someone else in the same company, (maybe even a cousin or their best friend). Now, they decide they're ready to join, but plan to sign up with that Rep, rather than the original one. The Rep who originally approached the business candidate feels like they have the *right* to sponsor them because they talked to them first. This, or some version of it, happens *a lot*. Sometimes it can get even more complicated than the way we've explained it. Just know that if you ever find yourself in this kind of situation, it's a smart idea to talk it through with someone in your upline who you trust will give you advice from a place of experience. In general though, would you really want to make someone join your team if they'd rather be somewhere else? Do the right thing and take the high road; it will always pay off.

EVERYONE SHOULD HAVE THE "RIGHT" TO CHOOSE THE SPONSOR THEY FEEL MOST COMFORTABLE WITH AND FEEL MOST LOYAL TO.

YOU'RE NEVER GIVEN A DREAM
WITHOUT ALSO BEING
GIVEN THE POWER TO
MAKE IT TRUE.

RICHARD BACH

CHAPTER FIVE

IT'S TIME TO LOOK IN THE MIRROR

Desire

de·sire / də'zi(ə)r/ *verb*: Strongly wish for or want (something).

Burning Desire

burn·ing / 'bərnīNG/ *adjective*: Very keenly or deeply felt; intense

BURNING DESIRE MINDSET = "YOUR WHY"

TWO FUNDAMENTAL REQUIREMENTS OF A SUCCESSFUL NM BUSINESS IN A BOX: DESIRE AND BELIEF

1. A sincere *desire* to have something you want, and a mindset that you won't give up until you get it, "no matter what." Something you want so badly you won't stop till you get it. That may sound trite, but it's probably **the single most important ingredient to your success**. Without a burning desire, most peeps just won't put up with the discomfort long enough to experience the rewards.

2. *Belief* in these four areas:
    1. Belief in Network Marketing
    2. Belief in the Company
    3. Belief in the Products
    4. Belief in Yourself

a crack in your belief, though, is like kryptonite to Superman.

When you have a strong belief in all four of these areas—and a no-matter-what attitude—you'll have discovered the secret to success in this business.

MAKING THE LEAP: 9-TO-5 EMPLOYEE TO NM ENTREPRENEUR

By doing your due diligence, you'll undoubtedly gain the confidence in the profession of NM, and will choose the right products and company to represent. The next important contributing factor to your success that you'll need to consider is *you*.

Let us explain what we mean by that.

Ultimately, you're the only one who knows whether or not you believe that you can really *do* this business. We won't sugarcoat it: success in NM takes a heck of a lot of determination, commitment of your time and energy, and consistent action. And the truth is that many people have considered what you're considering right now, made the decision to join a company, and then given up long before they ever achieved success.

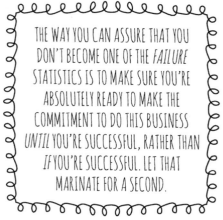

THE WAY YOU CAN ASSURE THAT YOU DON'T BECOME ONE OF THE *FAILURE* STATISTICS IS TO MAKE SURE YOU'RE ABSOLUTELY READY TO MAKE THE COMMITMENT TO DO THIS BUSINESS *UNTIL* YOU'RE SUCCESSFUL, RATHER THAN *IF* YOU'RE SUCCESSFUL. LET THAT MARINATE FOR A SECOND.

Mindset

mind·set / ˈmīn(d)set/ *noun:* The established set of attitudes held by someone.

To help you continue to assess the "you factor" of the equation, consider these five characteristics:

The 5 Characteristics of an Entrepreneurial Mindset

1. **Self-Reliant**

    You're responsible and fully committed. Shoot, if your picture were in the dictionary, it'd be found next to desire, drive, discipline, and determination. You don't just sit around waiting for things to happen; you go out and *make* them happen.

As an entrepreneur, you're the one who's running the show. Every decision from mega to miniscule falls on you. If that sounds like a lot of pressure, don't freak out. Simply understanding your expenses, your income, and your profit or loss and how they equate to the kind of activity you need to be in will help keep you on the right track. Think of your numbers as your guiding light—stay familiar with them, take them out to dinner, and become best friends.

2. **Self-Directed**

    Rawr! You recognize opportunities and go get 'em with constant and consistent effort. You've not only mastered the ability to hold both short- and long-term visions simultaneously, you've also learned to think ahead and consider all of the potential pitfalls and opportunities that may lie around the corner when making uncertain decisions.

    Now's as good a time as ever for you to come to terms with the fact that what you do—or don't do—today, will impact your business three months, even five years down the line. You'll do yourself a favor if you wake up every morning and go to sleep every night with that as your mantra. Why, you ask? Because you're not an employee, you're not going to get fired, and no one is going to pat you on the back for being the best rule follower. As an entrepreneur, you shouldn't be interested in the status quo, you should be looking for ways to do things better. You think Steve Jobs achieved his success because he thought to himself, eh, paper and pens aren't that bad? The answer you're looking for here is: "heck no!" Adopt the mindset of looking at things globally, and always be on the lookout for your next big "ah ha."

3. **Self-Confidence and Courage**

Skin? Ha! More like a bullet-proof vest. You don't worry yourself with things like rejection and criticism because feeling uncomfortable is your "comfort zone." You eat haters and skeptics for breakfast. Yea, sure, sometimes you're a party of one because the peeps around you just don't get it, but better to be a party of one than just another sheep lost in the herd.

Mindset is one of the most critical elements of being a successful entrepreneur. Want to know the most critical element in the life of a *failing* entrepreneur? Bingo! Mindset as well. Inside that beautiful noggin of yours lies the future and the demise of your NM business. So think about what this business can give you. And then consider if there's any other way you're going to achieve that. I think we can both agree that you've spent enough time waiting for that winning lottery ticket.

IT'S TIME TO START BETTING ON YOURSELF.

4. Self-Motivated

You're in the business of taking initiative, and you're kind of a big deal. Complacent Carol you are not. You determine what needs to be done and you do it without excuses because excuses are for wimps. You know what you do or don't do now will have an impact on your business in the future, so you make learning and challenging yourself the story that never ends.

As an employee, you have a job description. As an entrepreneur, you do not. SPOILER ALERT: you're going to need and want to learn lots of new skills, skills that could look like everything from improving the way you communicate, to crafting your perfect presentation, or using unfamiliar technology. Remember, you're the boss and this is a wimp-free zone, so that means you gotta do what needs to be done, no matter what. No excuses. Sure, as an employee you could survive doing stuff you dislike because there's a salary to help you justify it. But as an entrepreneur, you're not in the business of surviving; you're in the business of thriving! So that's why it's important to represent something that you really believe in. When you do what you love, it never really feels like work. Not loving your biz means you won't want to make the effort of an entrepreneur, and you definitely won't have the energy required to build a successful NM business.

5. Self-Disciplined

Schedules, shmedules! You're willing to put in the hours required, you're flexible, and work well without a consistent timetable. You know that all paychecks are not created equal and you've ditched your old way of thinking when it comes to making moolah. You understand that successful entrepreneurs are underpaid in the beginning but overpaid for the rest of their lives. This is the opposite of employees and "sheepwalkers," (those who care more about conforming to rules than producing results).

Most people underestimate how long it will take to start earning an income when it comes to their NM biz. If you're working, please don't quit. It'll keep you from becoming desperate. We all know that we don't need anymore "stalker" network marketers out there to give this biz a bad rap, right? So the moral of this story is to start now and know the effort and energy you put in is going to come back to you tenfold if you can commit to doing this until you're successful.

> WE ENCOURAGE EVERYONE TO START THEIR NM BUSINESS ALONGSIDE OF WHATEVER THEY'RE CURRENTLY DOING TO PAY THE BILLS. SURE YOU MAY LOSE A COUPLE HOURS OF SLEEP A WEEK OR HAVE TO GIVE UP YOUR FAVORITE TV SHOW, BUT DOING IT THIS WAY GIVES YOU THE TIME TO GROW YOUR NM INCOME WHILE ENJOYING THE SAFETY NET OF A SALARY.

Your belief in your ability to do this business is definitely the most tricky, and where most people are challenged. Have you ever heard the quote by Henry Ford, "Whether you think you can, or you think you can't, you're right"? Well it's true. If you think you *might* be able to do this business, or you're still not quite sure but you're *hoping* you can, that's better than being a complete skeptic—but it's not good enough. If you want to be really successful you've got to identify any doubts and face them head on. Maybe you haven't found the right product yet. Does the company culture feel like home to you? If not, what's missing? Are you still uncomfortable with something about the profession of NM? If you're lacking the belief in *your* ability to be successful at this, what would it take to change that? Dig deep. Figure out what is missing. Then start looking around you. Look for someone who you admire and respect and talk to them about whatever it is that you still have doubts about. Ask for help. Because if you want this badly enough you will find a way to make it happen. When your belief is strong enough, the *how* will take care of itself.

For those who come into this business understanding the concepts and the basics of what's required to be successful in this profession—

NM IS THE PLACE WHERE UNSTOPPABLE PEOPLE THRIVE.

and can say with complete clarity and confidence, **"I can do that"**—this will be a magical experience. That's when you will become unstoppable.

There's nowhere in the 9-to-5 world where your belief and mindset are as critical to your success as they are here. In the 9-to-5 world your ability to get a job hinges upon degrees and experience. Resumes and connections. It's about choices you've made in the past. It's about your *history*.

The barrier granting entrance to that world is too high for a lot of people. For all kinds of different reasons. But NM is very different. This business is about your future. Those who want something badly enough can achieve it here. And, if you happen to be someone who does have a good resume and connections, you won't even believe how great the potential is in NM compared to the world of 9-to-5s. There are no glass ceilings. No politics or discrimination. This is a world where no one is

 left out, and the underdog can rise to the top! Success is all about being crystal clear about what you want to create, and having a burning desire to achieve it, because this is the light at the end of the tunnel that leads to whatever you've been looking for.

THIS BUSINESS IS LIKE HAVING A CHANCE TO HIT THE RESTART BUTTON.

Why

Why / (h)wī/ *adverb:* For what reason or purpose

There is one prerequisite, though. And it's the common denominator and foundation of every successful network marketing business, big or small. It's called your why, and it's something that might sound a little woo-woo to most 9-to-5ers, but since it's ultimately the driving force of your success, please stay with us as we walk you through this.

YOUR EXPERIENCE AND CREDENTIALS ARE WHAT MATTER MOST IN THE 9-TO-5 WORLD. YOUR "WHY," MINDSET, STRONG DESIRE, SOLID BELIEF, AND STAYING POWER ARE THE SECRET SAUCE TO SUCCESS IN A NM BUSINESS.

when the "why" is big enough you will figure out "how"

"who" you'll share it with.

belief in "what" you're sharing.

your "why" is the foundation of your biz.

HOW
WHO
WHAT
WHY

YOUR WHY IS SOMETHING YOU WANT SO BADLY THAT JUST THINKING ABOUT IT MIGHT MAKE YOU REACH FOR THE TISSUES.

BELIEF IN SELF = YOUR DESIRE = *YOUR WHY*

"What exactly is a *why*" you ask, and "what makes it such a big deal?" In a nutshell, your why is something you passionately wish for, but have no idea how you'll get from "here to there." It's something that in your wildest dreams, you know you deserve, and you know you'll never stop dreaming about it, until you've achieved it. It's *your* unique reason for getting into NM—and you **definitely** need one. When most people start thinking about their why, they come up with all sorts of practical reasons for wanting to earn more money or having more free time. But practical reasons—no matter how valid—aren't strong enough to keep you in the game when the going gets tough. Trust us on this one.

To get beyond your practical reasons might take a little time. It requires digging deep. Look for those things that you secretly dream about. Something maybe no one else even knows you want. When you've found the why that makes you cry, that's when you know you've found *it*! That's your *big* why…"The why that makes you cry." Clever, right? Go ahead, you can tweet that.

> IF YOU EVER FIND YOURSELF TRYING TO FIGURE OUT WHY YOU'RE NOT ACHIEVING THE SUCCESS YOU BELIEVE YOU DESERVE IN THIS BUSINESS, YOU MIGHT WANT TO GO BACK TO EACH OF THE FOUR AREAS OF BELIEF TO FIND THE CRACK THAT'S KEEPING YOU FROM WHERE YOU ARE TO WHERE YOU WANT TO BE.

Most people in 9-to-5 land never stop to think about *why* they go to work every day. In fact, they might even start to worry about you if you asked them that question. It's such a given to most people, that going to work is just something you have to do, they never stop to think about it. Most people fall somewhere between; "I don't have any other choice," and "I absolutely love what I do." But, the reality is that the vast majority of people are "sheepwalking," going through the motions of the day without even noticing the world around them. Just look at the traffic on freeways any given weekday morning or evening, you'll find a sea of humans following the car in front of them, aimlessly lulled into accepting their fate.

Well, we're here to tell you that just because everyone's doing it doesn't mean it's the right thing to do, or that it's your *only* choice. Do you remember when you were little and your mom asked if you'd jump off a bridge just because everyone else was doing it?

Most people are jumping off the bridge just because someone else is. Don't jump off that bridge!

If you're here reading this book because you *have* been starting to feel like there must be more to life, and you're tired of feeling like a lemming, this is your chance to step back and think about what you'd like to change. You may already know your why. But if you're not, and you've never really thought about it before, now is the time to start. Because having a strong desire for something *different* is one of the most important components to your success in this biz. Especially when the light bulb goes on, and you suddenly realize that you've finally found a real way to achieve it.

Your emotional attachment to the vision of what you want serves as a constant reminder that what you do today will be worth the effort and sacrifices you make along the way. It's a little bit like that picture that's hanging on your refrigerator of you rockin' the cute bikini.

It's time to envision what you want your life to look like. The more committed you are to creating what you want, the more non-negotiable it becomes. You're heading into a non-traditional zone, and it's always going to mess with your mind when you go against the flow. Being on the cutting-edge of change takes courage. You have to be strong.

Making the leap from the 9-to-5 lifestyle to that of a NMer is a huge adjustment. It starts by **deciding** that you're not willing to settle for an ordinary life, and that you are committed to having an *extraordinary* one—even if everyone else thinks you've gone crazy.

No matter how ridiculously out of reach or unattainable your *why* might seem to all of your friends, family, or neighbors…who cares! This is *your* life. Why would you listen to anyone who isn't living a life that you'd want to live? A NM Business in a Box gives people new hope, and a way to move beyond where they are. So if you're going to go to all of the effort of seriously changing your life and freaking out your friends and fam, you might as well make it worthwhile, right?

WHAT IF YOU DON'T HAVE A BIG WHY?

For some peeps, dreaming big can be a tough assignment. Your why might be something you're not even consciously aware of, yet. But, for those whose life is really, really *not* working the way it is, taking the next steps to get a NM biz going will be much easier for you. The more motivated you are to changing your situation, the easier it will be for you to get started. If your life is pretty good, and there's nothing that's really "broken," you might just be so comfortable that the timing isn'l quite right for you at this point. Timing is everything in this profession. As long as you're already reading this, though…here are a few questions to get you started thinking:

ARE YOU PREPARED FOR IMPACT?

- How would your life be financially if the economy changes… again?
- Could you easily handle the extra expense if your car broke down, or your roof collapsed? Do you have the extra funds to take care of an emergency?
- What if you or someone you love is in an accident or becomes ill. Would you have the time and financial freedom to handle that situation the way you'd want to?

The challenge with being too comfortable is that most people

MONEY ISN'T EVERYTHING, FOR SURE, BUT IT DOES GIVE YOU MORE CHOICES.

don't think about needing a back-up plan until it's too late. Maybe you've been settling for so long that you've given up on dreaming. Or you might be someone who feels guilty asking for more when you have so much.

Everyone's dreams are different. One person might need an extra couple hundred dollars so their son can play soccer. Or maybe they'd just like to be able to eat out a few times a week. Someone else might just want the peace of mind of knowing there's a little extra instead of *not enough* money at the end of the month. Others are fortunate enough to already have all they need, but the reason they're attracted to this business could be the desire to help others have what they have. That's what this business offers that a 9-to-5 doesn't; this could be a means for you to help someone else turn their life around. It doesn't have to be just about you. Maybe you've always secretly dreamed of funding a cause you deeply believe in so you can make a difference in the world!

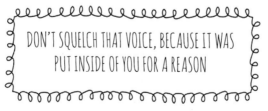

DON'T SQUELCH THAT VOICE, BECAUSE IT WAS PUT INSIDE OF YOU FOR A REASON

Whatever you're thinking right now, those thoughts are there for a reason. No matter how impossible your dreams might seem, if there's an idea inside of you that's just begging to be heard, listen to it.

from Lory and Janine

We appreciate you taking the time to gain a little more insight about a NM Business in a Box. It is our passion to create a *clarity movement* about what this business is, and what it is not. Unfortunately, too many people get into NM for the wrong reasons, with unrealistic expectations, and end up giving up without ever really treating it as a business. When that happens, every person in the NM profession loses, because that scenario feeds the myths and perpetuates the confusion. The more we unite as a profession to define what being an authentic network marketer entails, the sooner we will raise the bar and change the paradigm.

We know that this biz is definitely not the right fit for everyone, but for some, it's exactly what they've been searching for. Those are the people we hope will find this business. And for those who don't feel the need to free their toes, at least we hope you have a little more clarity about what a NM business encompasses. Maybe it's made you feel more inspired to support someone you know in their business. Or maybe you're thinking of someone who needs to know about this.

If, after reading this book, you happen to be one of the lucky ones who have decided that *you can do this*, we cannot encourage you enough to trust yourself, and take the next steps! If you choose this path and treat your Business in a Box with the integrity and respect it deserves, you are in for a huge awakening about what's possible. I would never have found NM had it not been for my daughter. I was not searching for free toes. I wasn't a dreamer, and didn't believe that it was possible to live life this way. I was Lory's biggest "Dream Stealer". Not because I wanted to hold her back, but because I was trying to protect her. I am so grateful that she didn't listen to me, and that she trusted her own voice above all others. I cannot imagine ever going back to the life I lived before. It's become my mission to share what I've found with others. Not everyone is looking for the light at the end of the tunnel, but for those who are, I want to be that messenger of hope, possibility and abundance.

Lory & Janine

A SELF-ASSESSMENT. AM I READY?

1. Are you willing to step outside your comfort zone?
2. Do you tend to be compliant (do what is expected of you) or committed (do what is needed to get the job done)?
3. Is the TIMING right?
4. Are your EXPECTATIONS in check?
5. Are you good at following a recipe, or do you need to create your own?
6. Are you ready to create MOMENTUM?
7. Are you EXCITED to share what you've found with others? If not…what will give you the confidence that you're missing?
8. Are you good at working with others?
9. Are you good at empowering others?
10. Can you handle rejection?
11. Do you need instant gratification?
12. Are you still tied to your image, title, or what it says on your business card?

Give yourself extra credit if (these aren't necessary, but helpful):
1. You know a lot of people
2. You find it easy to talk to strangers
3. You have excellent communication skills
4. You are successful in life
5. You have a strong network

Is your DESIRE so strong that you won't quit, no matter what?

Is your BELIEF strong enough in each of these areas:
- The products?
- The company?
- The profession of network marketing?
- Yourself?

LISTEN TO YOUR
HEART ABOVE ALL
OTHER VOICES.

MARTA KAGAN

IN THE NEXT SECTION OF THE BOOK,
YOU'LL FIND CAREER COMPARISONS FROM REAL LIVE,
FLIP FLOP CEO®'S, WHO'VE TRADED THEIR WORK SHOES FOR FLIP FLOPS,
AND WANT TO HELP YOU UNDERSTAND THE SIMILARITIES
AND THE DIFFERENCES BETWEEN WHAT THEY DID BEFORE,
AND WHAT THEY ARE DOING NOW.

5TH GRADE TEACHER COMPARED TO A FLIP FLOP CEO®

AMME WEILERT
5th Grade Teacher

What have you found to be the biggest differences between your previous career and NM?

The ability to create financial freedom along with time freedom—not just for our family, but to pay it forward to countless others.

What things are the same in your previous career and NM?

It requires the same ability to develop people. I love that teaching allowed me to hone those skills that transferred so easily to NM.

What new skills have you had to learn for NM that you didn't need in your previous career?

Resilience and to not take things personally. Also that anyone can successfully do NM, but not everyone will.

What skills from your previous career have helped you most in NM?

Helping to teach different personalities how to simply do something successfully! As a former teacher, I worked with all different types of children and personalities and I believe this prepared me for NM!

Compared to your previous career, what do you most appreciate about NM?

That I now get the choice to raise my own babies and not pay someone to raise them while I taught other people's children.

Compared to your previous career, what have you found to be the most challenging about NM?

Because it's not a 9-to-5, people sometimes think they don't need to do something everyday to grow a successful business with NM.

What do you consider to be the most important factor to achieving success in NM?

Building up your belief, doing at least one thing daily for your business, and staying the course until you succeed…and then staying the course to help others get there, too!

What advice would you give to someone coming into NM with a background similar to yours?

I believe teachers can do really great in NM because they already know how to successfully teach multiple personalities to do something very simply.

REGISTERED NURSE COMPARED TO A FLIP FLOP CEO®

SARA MARBLE
Registered Nurse

What have you found to be the biggest differences between your previous career and NM?

Network marketing has allowed me to build the life of my dreams. We are able to choose how to spend our time based on our priorities. As a wife and mom, that means more to me than anything. No more 12-hour night shifts away from my family. No more weekends and holidays at the hospital, missing out on what mattered most to me. No bosses dictating when I would have time to schedule vacations. I'm my own boss and can work when I want, and make it fit the life that I love.

What things are the same in your previous career and NM?

I always knew I wanted to be a nurse. I decided when I was eight, and never once changed my mind. It was my passion and heart's desire to help people. Network marketing has shown me you don't have to work in a hospital to have the opportunity to help people. Partnering with a health and wellness company has given me the chance to touch people's lives in a way I never knew I could. Sharing the business opportunity has allowed so many people to experience financial freedom as well. I never dreamed I would feel so fulfilled and able to help just as many people outside of the hospital, as in it. What an amazing thing to experience truly changing lives, both as a nurse and network marketer.

What new skills have you had to learn for NM that you didn't need in your previous career?

Leadership skills would have to be the biggest thing I had to learn to be successful in network marketing. I had no clue what I was doing. It took a while for me to realize I needed some personal growth and development if I was going to go far. Learning how to be a good leader has been essential for me since retiring from my nursing job. As a nurse, I would punch in, do my job, and punch out, never really thinking about any type of leadership roll. As a network marketer, good leadership skills are critical and necessary to achieve big goals and dreams.

What skills from your previous career have helped you most in NM?

People skills! Learning how to talk to anyone and everyone. Learning to sympathize, empathize, and listen are all things that helped me be a good nurse, and have definitely carried over to my network marketing business.

Compared to your previous career, what do you most appreciate about NM?

Time freedom! Financial freedom! The ability to set my own schedule and choose each day how to spend my time.

Compared to your previous career, what have you found to be the most challenging about NM?

Working from home and being my own boss has proven challenging as far as time management and learning how to delegate and allot time to things. Business hours blur into family time and vice versa and I have to regularly evaluate and balance how I manage my time to be the most effective mommy and network marketer I can be.

What do you consider to be the most important factor to achieving success in NM?

Being coachable is key to being successful. I value all of the people who taught me so much. Personal growth and development has also been essential. Reading, listening, and associating with positive, supportive, and inspiring friends, family, and mentors has helped to shape me into the person I have become on this network marketing journey.

What advice would you give to someone coming into NM with a background similar to yours?

I would say don't over think things. Coming from a medical background can sometimes make people overly skeptical when it comes to products, and even an alternative way to earn an income. Network marketing is our plan B that very quickly became our plan A when we realized it truly was a better way to live our life. After diving in head first and never looking back, all of our dreams for our life are coming true.

LAWYER AND PUBLIC RELATIONS EXECUTIVE COMPARED TO A FLIP FLOP CEO®
ROMI NEUSTADT
Lawyer, Public Relations Executive

What have you found to be the biggest differences between your previous career and NM?

I was tied to the billable hour. NM offers a residual income in which customers continue to purchase products from us, and our organizations grow while we sleep. I also love that in NM there's no glass ceiling. With the wage gap between men and women alive and well in the U.S.—and a lack of leadership positions still prevalent in large law firms and PR agencies—it's so exciting to know that as a woman, I can earn as much as I want and that my leadership potential is unlimited. Equally important is the ability to design a life with balance, which is something I didn't often see in law or PR, especially if you're juggling kids.

What things are the same in your previous career and NM?

In law and PR, I told stories. I don't think most people think of law that way, but that's what we're trained to do. A good brief or courtroom argument communicates facts. A great one connects emotionally with the jury and helps them see the case through their own eyes and experiences. And the greatest network marketers connect the benefits of their business and products or services with the lives, hopes, and dreams of the prospect.

In PR I told stories too, but the thing from that profession that is most similar to network marketing is the requirement to be tenacious. I was used to pitching a story to a number of editors, writers, and producers to get my clients publicity. And I would get "no"s…lots of "no"s. But I learned that if I kept going— leading with what's in it for the news outlet and its readers or viewers—I would find the those who wanted to feature my clients. It's the same in NM. Connect with your prospects. Let your words paint the picture of them benefitting from your products or business. And don't let the "no"s slow you down.

What new skills have you had to learn for NM that you didn't need in your previous career?

I didn't have to learn any new skills; I was able to apply my existing skill sets to my new profession. But I did have to learn a new mindset. Because of NM, I am now a recovered control freak. As a young associate lawyer, as long as I worked hard, I could control the outcome of my work product. As a PR pro, I was in control of developing and executing campaigns. And I could control the work product of the people I supervised, since they were employees, and were at risk of being fired for poor performance.

In NM, I can't control what my business partners do. They are independent contractors and I can't make them do anything. And I can't control how my prospects will respond. All I can control is myself and what I consistently do every day to build my business and serve our customers and our team.

What skills from your previous career have helped you most in NM?

My two previous careers involved a lot of talking. A lot of storytelling. And I had to do both in a concise and compelling way. I also learned how to cut through extraneous BS and get to the point. Listening was also a big part of what I did—to clients, to judges, to colleagues, to media professionals—in order to better understand how I could be helpful, effective, and compelling. And resilience was imperative for law and PR, because there were challenges, disappointments, unexpected turns of events, and long hours. All of this has served me incredibly well in my NM career.

Compared to your previous career, what do you most appreciate about NM?

I had two careers that were ruled by the billable hour and required me to be at the beck and call of my clients. While I enjoyed being of service to my clients, not owning my own time became increasingly frustrating after I became a mom. The NM profession allowed me to build a lucrative business on my terms. I often say that we have the ability to design a professional life that fits in around the rest of our life, instead of the other way around.

Compared to your previous career, what have you found to be the most challenging about NM?

Working with a team comprised of all independent contractors who set their own business hours and own goals in the business has been the most challenging. From day one, I treated NM as a business. I was coachable and consistent, and fit my NM business in everywhere I could. My goal was big—to set myself free from Corporate America and to provide financial and time freedom for myself and my family. But the reality is, most people don't have that same goal. And that's OK. But when I was first starting out, I assumed everyone would want what I wanted. The most challenging part was realizing and accepting that unlike in corporations, everyone creates their own goals and that people have very different motivations for building their NM businesses.

What do you consider to be the most important factor to achieving success in NM?

I wholeheartedly believe that people succeed or fail in NM because of their mindset. It's not because of their educational or professional pedigrees. And there are enough outstanding resources to teach us how to do what we do. What's between our ears dictates how we think, act, and feel. Developing a positive, success-and-growth mindset is crucial. There are many wonderful resources inside and outside NM for personal development to help us all continue to grow and stretch.

What advice would you give to someone coming into NM with a background similar to yours?

People who have had high-powered corporate careers—especially if they've been managing teams—would benefit from simply opening their minds and committing to being 100% coachable. Each company has a system that helps its business builders maximize the compensation plan. No matter how successful you've been in your previous career/s, understand that you need to learn how to do this. Leave any arrogance at the door and learn how to build your own business and how to coach and inspire others to do the same. And just like in law or PR, you've got to consistently show up with discipline and determination. It's no different in NM, even if it's only a little bit every day.

SMALL BUSINESS OWNER COMPARED TO A FLIP FLOP CEO®

KAREN DOERFLEIN
Small Business Owner

What have you found to be the biggest differences between your previous career and NM?

When I had my traditional business, I had always said; what business can you do with no overhead and employees? My previous business was a 9,000 square foot retail space with seventeen employees (at the height of the market), and a $90,000 a month break even. With my network marketing business I have no overhead, no employees, and no inventory.

What things are the same in your previous career and NM?

Success with any business requires dedication, work ethic, and a long-term vision. Traditional business and network marketing are both businesses. When I joined network marketing, I treated it as if I paid $500,000 to start it, not $499.

What new skills have you had to learn for NM that you didn't need in your previous career?

Skills that I have developed in network marketing: I have become a better listener. I have learned to understand people more, and I've learned more about how to be better at empowering others.

What skills from your previous career have helped you most in NM?

Having a traditional business helped me know that there would be highs and lows and that you must continue to push through and have a big-picture vision of what the future holds, not just the present circumstances. Knowing that all businesses are a numbers and sorting game. I would have to make calls and connect with people for sales in my previous company and it's the same in network marketing. Know that the more people you speak with, the faster you will grow your business.

Compared to your previous career, what do you most appreciate about NM?

I most appreciate the freedom and the ability to start on a very part-time basis. When I started in network marketing eight years ago, I was working 80 hours a week with three small children. I loved that I could do something very part time and create a residual income stream. Also the freedom to travel with our family and work the business from anywhere. The past two years we have lived in Bali, Indonesia, and have traveled with our kids to eight countries while my business grew. I also love that it's a business that can be passed to future generations.

Compared to your previous career, what have you found to be the most challenging about NM?

The most challenging thing about network marketing is that not everyone is going to see the opportunity. In my opinion, people quit too soon and really do not have long-term vision. They go back to living paycheck to paycheck, doing things they don't like, and settling for "existing" instead of creating an incredible life with choices.

What do you consider to be the most important factor to achieving success in NM?

Long-term vision and commitment. The quote "without vision people will perish" rings very true in this business. I tell people you have to give this business at least 3-5 years, not three months. Most people committed to college for four years and, in many cases, that has not served them in what they are currently doing in their jobs.

What advice would you give to someone coming into NM with a background similar to yours?

If you've previously owned your own small business, treat this business like a traditional business and not a hobby. Dedicate and commit to it like any other business and be "all in" from the beginning. If you treat it like a "side thing" or just "trying it out," you will not attract serious people into your business and it will be harder to paint the vision of what is possible with this business.

CORPORATE SALES COMPARED TO A FLIP FLOP CEO®

SUZANNE VAN PARYS
Corporate Sales/Sales Management

What have you found to be the biggest differences between your previous career and NM?

One of the biggest differences is how personal it feels when people say no. Even though in my corporate career, my job was to build relationships with my clients when they said no, it didn't feel as personal. When you start NM, you approach friends and family first—your "warm" market—but often they're the most chilly and aren't as enthusiastic about our new venture as you thought they'd be. This is something we learn to deal with and view as part of our process and journey to success, and handling these "no"s and moving on is key.

Another key difference is the support/encouragement/mentorship that isn't really a part of the corporate world like it is in NM. Once a company provides training in the corporate world, you're typically on your own. In NM, you feel like someone always has your best interests at heart. Even though the goal is to help develop people as leaders and to be independent, there's always support at every stage of one's journey.

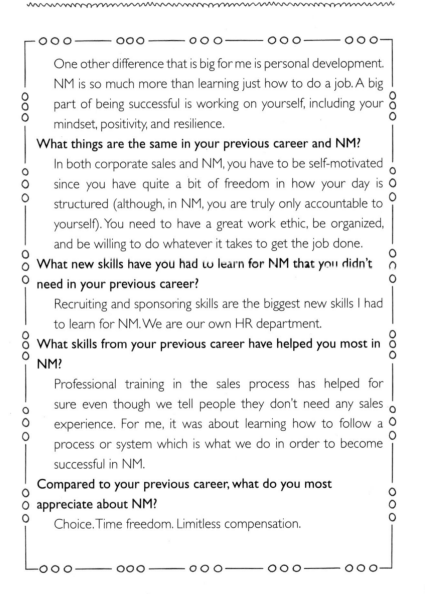

One other difference that is big for me is personal development. NM is so much more than learning just how to do a job. A big part of being successful is working on yourself, including your mindset, positivity, and resilience.

What things are the same in your previous career and NM?

In both corporate sales and NM, you have to be self-motivated since you have quite a bit of freedom in how your day is structured (although, in NM, you are truly only accountable to yourself). You need to have a great work ethic, be organized, and be willing to do whatever it takes to get the job done.

What new skills have you had to learn for NM that you didn't need in your previous career?

Recruiting and sponsoring skills are the biggest new skills I had to learn for NM. We are our own HR department.

What skills from your previous career have helped you most in NM?

Professional training in the sales process has helped for sure even though we tell people they don't need any sales experience. For me, it was about learning how to follow a process or system which is what we do in order to become successful in NM.

Compared to your previous career, what do you most appreciate about NM?

Choice. Time freedom. Limitless compensation.

Compared to your previous career, what have you found to be the most challenging about NM?

Learning how to inspire others. It's not about motivation because that has to come from within. But because we aren't anybody's boss, they don't have to do what we say (even though it's what's going to help them be successful). We have to learn to inspire others to believe in themselves and dig deep to find what motivates them to keep going to achieve success. We also need to inspire by example—leading from the front.

What do you consider to be the most important factor to achieving success in NM?

Grit—the passion and perseverance to keep going no matter what. To be consistent and practice every day. Most people underestimate what they can accomplish in five years and overestimate what they can accomplish in one. View this business as a five-year business plan and stick with it!

What advice would you give to someone coming into NM with a background similar to yours?

Be coachable and open. You don't already know everything. Invest in your personal development every day and work on yourself. Your business will grow as big as you do.

CHIROPRACTOR COMPARED TO A FLIP FLOP CEO®

SCOTT SCHULER
Chiropractor

What have you found to be the biggest differences between your previous career and NM?

A couple of things come to mind immediately. When I was in practice, the only way I made money was seeing individual patients. Granted, other modalities we had in the clinic made us money when I wasn't actively adjusting patients, but as an owner, if I took a vacation or wasn't in the office, my income went down considerably. As you build your business with NM, you have the opportunity to see little to no interruption in income when you take time off. Also for the majority of patients, coming into the clinic at 8:45PM was not a convenient option. NM gives you the opportunity to choose when you work.

What things are the same in your previous career and NM?

Although many try to say NM gives you complete time freedom, insinuating you hardly have to work at all isn't accurate. The time freedom this business gives you is the ability to make the choice about when and where you work. Just like any other business, you get out of it what you put into it. Work this business like a hobby and you'll get paid like a hobby. Work it like a real business and you have the chance to make real money.

What new skills have you had to learn for NM that you didn't need in your previous career?

I am going to say something that may be a little controversial. I don't believe there is a difference for any occupation regarding the skills needed to be successful. Andy Andrews talks in his book, *The Noticer*, about how opportunities and encouragement come from people, and in order to receive these opportunities and encouragement from people, they have to want to be around you. Life and this business in particular are all about relationships and if no one wants to be around you, you're going to struggle.

What skills from your previous career have helped you most in NM?

I had to learn real quick how to talk to people, get past their salesman filter, and put my recommendations in a language they could understand and process.

Compared to your previous career, what do you most appreciate about NM?

When I was in practice, there was a definitive ceiling on the number of people I could directly impact and help in a day. With the NM model, I have infinite leverage because I can teach other people how to help and indirectly impact the lives of countless others.

Compared to your previous career, what have you found to be the most challenging about NM?

The hardest thing has been shutting down. With this age of technology at our fingertips, you could literally do this business anywhere, anytime. I have to make a conscious effort to turn off and unplug, making sure the rest of my life doesn't get to out of balance. This is not to say that there are definitely seasons of hustle and putting your nose to the grindstone, but you also have to take the time to fill your own soul so you can be there for those closest to you. You can't give what you don't have.

What do you consider to be the most important factor to achieving success in NM?

Being in consistent action in all areas, recruitment, and self-improvement. Also giving back. If you look at the most successful people in this industry, they are not only consistently taking action but they are also givers. They are always giving to their team and the profession.

What advice would you give to someone coming into NM with a background similar to yours?

The beginning is tough. We coach our team about how fishing from two boats (doing multiple NM companies) is a losing proposition, but when you are in the transition phase you are fishing from the job boat and NM boat. That time in the beginning has a higher emphasis on the job but, over time as you take consistent action, you'll begin to see a change in that emphasis take place. The difference between success and failure are those who continue versus those who quit.

PHARMACEUTICAL REP COMPARED TO A FLIP FLOP CEO®

VIDA ICE
Hospital Based Pharmaceutical Rep

What have you found to be the biggest differences between your previous career and NM?

Time freedom! Balance.

What things are the same in your previous career and NM?

Account management, cultivating advocates, leadership and training, health education, product knowledge, sales, interpersonal skills, and influencing someone to take action.

What new skills have you had to learn for NM that you didn't need in your previous career?

Dealing with what others will think, dealing with non-professionals, understanding passive income, and how to leverage time. I've also had to learn how to budget my own finances because I didn't have an expense budget from corporate. I've learned to lead people, rather than manage them. Other new skills include: creating vision, learning longer term goal setting, utilizing the power of social media, and empowering and coaching individuals.

What skills from your previous career have helped you most in NM?

Handling rejection, overcoming objections, being a professional, goal setting, business analysis, cultivating relationships, and sales techniques.

Compared to your previous career, what do you most appreciate about NM?

I appreciate the flexibility and portability of this business. I enjoy helping others succeed, giving them the recognition they deserve, helping them find their purpose in life, become healthy, and how to use this vehicle to follow their passions. Teaching people how to create balance in their lives, and being part of something bigger than myself.

Compared to your previous career, what have you found to be the most challenging about NM?

Since there really aren't any prerequisites to this business, other than being 18 years old, and a legal citizen, we get all kinds of people who join this business. I love the diversity, but while we attract people who see the bigger picture—and are willing to put in the work—we also attract those who are looking for a quick fix. The biggest challenge is discerning who to spend time working with. Since this is a person's own business, influencing them to follow a proven system is very challenging when they want to do things their own way. I find this to be a big challenge for those who have worked in Corporate America and want to be looked at as the expert so they stand out, and feel like they need to know every little thing before they even get started. Also, since we are responsible for our time each day, one of the most challenging things is managing the distractions that vie for our attention.

What do you consider to be the most important factor to achieving success in NM?

Developing a strong vision, and treating the profession like a business with tremendous income potential.

What advice would you give to someone coming into NM with a background similar to yours?

I would say be willing to be coached in all areas of this business. Follow the system that is already proven to work. Don't try to make your position more important than it is. The key is to follow a simple, duplicable system so others can easily follow, instead of being so polished that people come up to you in awe of your presentation and then say, "I can't do what you do." And most of all, learn to love people where they're at.

FLIGHT ATTENDANT COMPARED TO A FLIP FLOP CEO®

HOPE BAKER
Flight Attendant

What have you found to be the biggest differences between your previous career and NM?

Although I loved flying, my career in network marketing allows me to be my own boss and build the life I've dreamed of! As with most jobs, as a flight attendant, I traded time for money, and was only paid when I walked through the airplane door. With network marketing, I have the ability to earn residual income and, through this industry, I've been able to achieve amazing financial success that simply wouldn't have been possible otherwise. More importantly, network marketing has given me the ability to "pay it forward" and change other people's lives for the better.

This industry gives us all an opportunity to have a really positive impact on the world, one person and one family at a time. Being able to make a significant contribution like that is so personally rewarding, and one of the best parts of what we do!

What things are the same in your previous career and NM?

The similarity between being a flight attendant and network marketing lays in two words: loving People! As a flight attendant,

I found those who truly loved their jobs, including myself, really loved people. Loving and wanting to help people is one of the biggest components of network marketing, too. Happy flight attendants love working with people, love meeting them, love the uniqueness of everyone, and really enjoy developing relationships.

As network marketers, our job is connecting with all sorts of different people, forming meaningful relationships and being of service to people. Happily working with people is the common thread between working as a flight attendant and working in network marketing, and one of the best parts of both professions.

What new skills have you had to learn for NM that you didn't need in your previous career?

As I started my network marketing career, there were skills I realized I needed to work on if I was going to be successful. I needed to grow as a leader. I needed to expand my vision of what was possible and think beyond a paycheck! Because we're our own boss in network marketing, I also needed to learn how to manage my time. No one was telling me when I had to work. I had no "sign-in" time, so I needed to work smart and work with intention.

What skills from your previous career have helped you most in NM?

As a flight attendant, we were encouraged to reach out to

people and connect. Being friendly, thoughtful, and authentic are integral parts of network marketing, too. Developing the skill of working efficiently is also important in both careers.

In the airline industry, you need to be efficient to get your job done between point A and point B. In network marketing, you want to work efficiently so you can get your work done and enjoy the life you're building.

Compared to your previous career, what do you most appreciate about NM?

I loved being a flight attendant for the adventure, travel, and social nature of the job. In network marketing, I enjoy those same things, but I now live my life by *my* design. I travel when I want, work with people I love, and am building a life without limits!

Compared to your previous career, what have you found to be the most challenging about NM?

The most challenging part of network marketing—at least at the beginning—is realizing that we all have the power to create exactly what we want. Most people need to expand their vision and understand what's possible! It's easy to forget that we are all where we are today because of the decisions we made yesterday. In network marketing, we can do and be whatever and whoever we choose to be!

What do you consider to be the most important factor to achieving success in NM?

The most important factors in succeeding in network marketing are belief and determination!

Belief in yourself, belief in this incredible industry, and belief in what's possible...coupled with determination to make this business whatever you want it to be!

What advice would you give to someone coming into NM with a background similar to yours?

To all of the interesting, energetic, fun-loving, and fabulous flight attendants out there searching for something more—I'd so encourage you to jump into network marketing with gusto! For most, I think it would be such a natural fit and you'd have fun and grow in ways you never thought possible.

NUTRITIONAL COUNSELOR COMPARED TO A FLIP FLOP CEO®

BARBARA BEATY, PhD
Nutritional Counselor

What have you found to be the biggest differences between your previous career and NM?

Time freedom. As a nutritional counselor, I spent hours at the office meeting with clients and even more time after hours creating personalized plans. In addition to long days, I was confined to my office; I felt confined physically and financially. Today I take my business with me. It goes wherever I go, and I make my own schedule. I work as little or as much as I want to. If I want to take a day off, a week off, or even a month off, I can; and my income remains the same. Before starting my NM business, vacations consisted of two weeks a year. Today I take multiple vacations throughout the year. And most of them have been paid for by my company.

What things are the same in your previous career and NM?

I still help people take charge of their health with the products and nutritional plan offered through my company. Helping people become all they were created to be is really what NM is all about, and that's all I've ever really wanted to do.

What new skills have you had to learn for NM that you didn't need in your previous career?

I've learned the power of belief and intention. In a traditional career, you invest a certain amount of time and receive the equivalent in income. You're constantly exchanging time for money. Before I started my NM business, the term "dream big" was only a cliché. I could work night and day in my nutritional counseling practice and never achieve the financial success I've achieved in my network marketing business. In my nutritional counseling practice, I could only exchange so many hours for income. I could dream big, but never too big. Today the sky is truly the limit!

What skills from your previous career have helped you most in NM?

In NM, you quickly realize the potential for massive income with no glass ceiling. Knowing this intellectually is one thing, but embracing it for yourself is something entirely different. I had to believe this gig really worked. I had to believe if other people with less education and experience could do this, I certainly could do it too. I learned to be a visionary. I learned to set goals and achieve them. And I learned how to help other people do the same.

Compared to your previous career, what do you most appreciate about NM?

As a nutritional counselor, it was very important for me to learn to listen to my clients. My initial interview with them played a crucial role in developing their individualized plan. I learned early on that asking lots of questions and listening to prospects hopes, dreams, and even objections would help determine if NM was a good fit for them. It also helped me connect with the prospect on a deeper emotional level, which is key to success. The power of rapport can never be underestimated in this business.

Compared to your previous career, what have you found to be the most challenging about NM?

Financial freedom and time freedom. I don't know of another career that would allow me to create significant wealth on my terms. I was self-employed; but I also carried the headache that goes with business ownership.

What do you consider to be the most important factor to achieving success in NM?

Helping people to see that it really works. That's one of the reasons I'm such a big fan of THE *flip flop* CEO® It basically does all the hard work for you.

What advice would you give to someone coming into NM with a background similar to yours?

Don't over think it. This business is pretty straightforward. You share something you love with the people you care about, and they do the same. And don't think you have to know it all to get started. The best network marketers follow a simple system and make it look ridiculously simple. People don't care how much you know, they only want to know how much you care.

Most importantly, don't worry about what other people may think. You wouldn't care what other people thought of you if you realized how little they did. Most people are too caught up in their 9-to-5 chaos to be concerned about your life decisions. If anything, saying yes to this opportunity will most likely set other people free to do the same.

DENTAL HYGIENIST COMPARED TO A FLIP FLOP CEO®

KELLY MCALLISTER
Dental Hygienist

What have you found to be the biggest differences between your previous career and NM?

As a dental hygienist, I was on someone else's terms. I felt like there was no room for growth in the industry. No matter how hard I worked, I was never going to be promoted to dentist. My salary was capped. I was told once I was being paid the most they would ever pay a hygienist. I remember thinking if I ever wanted to make more money, I would have to take on more hours, which was not where I saw my life.

When I started NM, things were on my terms. I worked this into my already hectic life and knew if I worked this business hard, I would be rewarded for my efforts. Then I realized the tables had turned, and now I was the one in control of how much I made.

What things are the same in your previous career and NM?

In both industries it's really about helping other people. I feel my hygiene background has really helped me in NM.

What new skills have you had to learn for NM that you didn't need in your previous career?

Two big things I have learned are leadership and mentoring.

These are skills I never needed as a hygienist and have been so rewarding to learn.

My computer skills have also improved because of this business. Another area for me was presenting and training. I had no idea what a PowerPoint presentation was, let alone making one! I feel this industry has grown me in so many new directions. This business really has been one of the biggest educations of my life.

What skills from your previous career have helped you most in NM?

In both industries it's about selling. I find it funny when people tell me they don't sell. Think about it: we all sell everyday. As a hygienist, I was selling dentistry, toothbrushes, treatment and, most of all, myself.

As a mom, I sell eating healthy, taking baths, school, homework— you name it.

As a network marketer, I sell products and a business opportunity. I never saw myself as a "salesperson," but essentially as a hygienist…I was.

Compared to your previous career, what do you most appreciate about NM?

I now have time freedom and time flexibility. If I want a day off, all I need to do is ask my boss and I say to myself, "Sure take the day off." I no longer feel the "Sunday Night Blues" and dread Monday morning.

From a financial perspective, I now make more than the dentists I worked for. I never in a million years believed I would ever have that luxury. The best part? I built this business by helping other people. So not only am I financially rewarded, but knowing I've helped others achieve their dreams has been the most rewarding part of this entire profession.

Compared to your previous career, what have you found to be the most challenging about NM?

It's a business. In businesses there are ups and downs. When things are up in this business, it's great fun. When things take a dip, it requires managing your thoughts and not getting overly discouraged.

What do you consider to be the most important factor to achieving success in NM?

Commitment, consistency, and personal growth. You need to commit to the business and treat it like a multimillion dollar organization from day one. Commit to activity, learning and growing, and remove the option to quit. You need to be consistent. You can work this business part time, but not some-time. Commit to daily activity. Personal growth is mandatory. So much of this business is played out between our ears. We need to learn how to think like a pro!

What advice would you give to someone coming into NM with a background similar to yours?

My advice to any dental hygienists out there is to *jump in.* You have absolutely nothing to lose!

If you keep doing dental hygiene, where do you see yourself in 5-10 years? Or better yet, if you injured yourself and were unable to work, how long could you pay your bills? The dental industry has changed, and dental hygienists are not being compensated the way they used to.

Find a NM company that resonates with you. It may not be your "passion" initially, but eventually it will.

Whatever your dreams are for your life, you need a vehicle. This business is a vehicle to help you achieve your dream life. Follow their system for success, commit to your business, and get comfortable being uncomfortable at first. You will quickly learn that your comfort zone will grow…and so will you!

POLICE OFFICER COMPARED TO A FLIP FLOP CEO®

KEVIN BARNUM
Police Officer (Undercover Drug Officer/
Emergency Response Team/Canine Handler)

What have you found to be the biggest differences between your previous career and NM?

NM is about building relationships, understanding challenges (problems), and providing solutions. Time management is a must in NM; this is a proactive business model. As a police officer, most times it's reactive.

What things are the same in your previous career and NM?

People are very predictable. "How you do anything is how you do everything." You work on your own, but you are also a part of a team.

What new skills have you had to learn for NM that you didn't need in your previous career?

Listening more and being patient.

What skills from your previous career have helped you most in NM?

Reading people and being able to communicate effectively.

Compared to your previous career, what do you most appreciate about NM?

"Financial Freedom is Family Freedom" It was impossible to

attain financial freedom as a police officer. In less than 18 months, we had replaced over $250,000 in combined income.

Compared to your previous career, what have you found to be the most challenging about NM?

Meeting people where they are. This is a volunteer business and you must be a real leader for people to follow. Leadership is not built on a uniform or position but on caring about people and helping them accomplish their dreams!

What do you consider to be the most important factor to achieving success in NM?

Daily action—set a schedule and stick to it. In our case, when we started with the NM business model, we worked two hours a day, five days a week, and never missed a day. (A minimum of three new contacts and three follow-up calls everyday) *No excuses!*

What advice would you give to someone coming into NM with a background similar to yours?

Police officers are the most skeptical (often times negative) people to work with because of what they deal with on the street. Stay away from negativity; focus on learning and personal development. Be sure to look for like-minded officers who are always looking to earn more money. Perhaps they have rental properties, own a small business, or are into the stock market. Look for the go-getters who want out of the job, and see more than just a pension with medical benefits.

REAL ESTATE AGENT COMPARED TO A FLIP FLOP CEO®

KATHLEEN DEGGELMAN
Real Estate Agent
Sales & Marketing in Corporate America for 25 years

What have you found to be the biggest differences between your previous career and NM?

I think the biggest differences between my previous career and NM are the income potential, the time freedom, the fun factor, and the ability to work when and where I choose. And as long as I have internet, I truly can work from anywhere. I get to travel with my business, and I have friendships all over the world now. The headaches are different, too. Our company handles all the heavy lifting. We get to do the fun part—share the products, service, and opportunity. The company handles the rest!

What things are the same in your previous career and NM?

I have found that NM requires the same ability to build relationships with people, and also the fact that at the end of the day, my success is still up to me. Your efforts will equal your rewards…but the rewards in network marketing are greater than as an employee or owner of a small business.

What new skills have you had to learn for NM that you didn't need in your previous career?

What I had to learn was that instead of working independently as I did in real estate sales, it's critical in NM to know how to build a team and team culture, which can be a lot more fun. The way your team perceives the value they get from you can determine whether they stay or not.

What skills from your previous career have helped you most in NM?

It's been a big help to already have good people skills. I know how to build and keep relationships, and I'm good at getting along with and knowing how to make people feel appreciated. It's also helped to be disciplined and good at staying in consistent activity.

Compared to your previous career, what do you most appreciate about NM?

Comparing the two careers, what I most appreciate about NM is the time freedom to work when and where I choose, the friendships I have all over the world, and the ability to really make a difference in so many people's lives.

Compared to your previous career, what have you found to be the most challenging about NM?

What I find most challenging is remembering that you are dealing with human nature. And, unfortunately, sometimes people don't follow through or don't have the vision for their lives that I see. And I've needed to learn to make sure that I'm working with people who have earned my attention.

What do you consider to be the most important factor to achieving success in NM?

I believe the most important factor to achieving success in NM is being consistent, and staying focused and disciplined with the daily activities of introducing new people to what you have to offer. I have seen lots of people over the years quit too soon and that doesn't work in our business. A mentor told me years ago that the people who make the most money are the ones who spend the time and the years! We need to be careful of the "shiny penny syndrome."

What advice would you give to someone coming into NM with a background similar to yours?

To take the time to make sure you're choosing a company that will really work for you and will be around. Work with a great mentor—either someone in your company or outside. Put the time in. Set realistic expectations about how long it will take. Work on yourself through personal development courses because the business will grow as you do. Enjoy the journey and don't take it all too seriously. People will be attracted to the fun and the energy and the passion you share with them!

PERSONAL TRAINER COMPARED TO A FLIP FLOP CEO®

JACKIE CHRISTIANSEN
Personal Trainer & Sports Nutritionist

What have you found to be the biggest differences between your previous career and NM?

- Passive and residual income. When I had my training and nutrition business, I made money only if I had a client in front of me. In other words, when my clients were done with their appointment, the income left with them, so to speak. If I wanted to take some time off to vacation with my family, I lost money that week. If I was injured or sick and needed to take time off, I lost money as well because I wasn't training anyone. Also, my ability to leverage my time was very limited. In NM, if I take time off for vacation or I'm sick one day, my income doesn't change. In fact, I love the fact that I still make money (and sometimes more money) during the week or two I am on vacation at an exotic destination! The tools I have designed for my business also allow me to leverage my time so that I do the work once and my efforts (systems) are in place for the future needs of my growing team.

- I'm able to help a greater number of people at one time. It used to be that I was able to help one person at a time when

I was training or consulting with them. I'm now able to help a multitude of people all at once because they are using better products that improve their overall health.

What things are the same in your previous career and NM?

I'm still helping people improve the quality of their lives through health, but on a much larger scale.

What new skills have you had to learn for NM that you didn't need in your previous career?

It's a whole new skill set, but definitely worth the effort. Personal development plays a huge role in the success of your NM business and the more you invest in yourself, the greater the return will be. The technical skills related to your individual company and the industry can be easily learned, especially with a good sponsor or coach. What's great about it is that it's a "learn as you earn" scenario, and it's a level playing field; no special background or skills are needed to succeed.

What skills from your previous career have helped you most in NM?

Helping people reach a goal; motivating, coaching, and laying out a plan for their success. I love being able to teach people how to do this business and—with a willing and committed student—they will be successful in this industry as well. It also helped that I had my own company and had been my own boss. Learning to use your time wisely is key to productivity.

Compared to your previous career, what do you most appreciate about NM?

I appreciate the residual and passive income. I'm earning more money than I ever made as a trainer. I appreciate the time freedom and ability to make my own schedule, and to be in charge of my life. I love no longer being tied to swapping time for dollars. The lifestyle of having an international business allows my family and me to travel to other countries and experience their cultures and lifestyles. I love being able to see the world and write it off as a business expense.

What do you consider to be the most important factor to achieving success in NM?

It's so important to have the belief that you'll succeed. Be coachable, follow a plan and strategy for success, and persist until you succeed. Follow a good coach or mentor in your company or industry and follow their lead. Having a support system is so important. Belief + Success Plan + Action Over Time = Success!

What advice would you give to someone coming into NM with a background similar to yours?

Keep your focus on helping others, just like you do in your training business. Find the best company you can—one you can get behind, and excited about the products and mission of the company. If you're excited about your new mission, others will catch your fire and enthusiasm. Find a sponsor and team that will help, support, and teach you the skills you need. Use your business and interpersonal skills you have as a wellness professional to create the life you have always dreamed about.

ACTRESS AND SINGER COMPARED TO A FLIP FLOP CEO®

JULES PRICE
Professional Actress and Singer

What have you found to be the biggest differences between your previous career and NM?

In NM, you suddenly have actual rankings with activity/results numbers and tracking, versus in the performing world there is a very nebulous gray area of what constitutes "success." In NM, you can truly be the master of your own success and have a huge opportunity to get where you want to go if you do the work and follow the system, versus always waiting for someone else to put you up on stage or give you a shot. Another interesting difference is that in NM, the more you're able to succeed and be a part of other people's journeys, the more you feel fulfilled. In performing it's a lonely profession overall because it's ultimately all about you.

What things are the same in your previous career and NM?

In both professions, you have to have a strong vision, set goals, go after it despite obstacles that arise (and there are *many* obstacles that arise!), and belief in yourself—whether anyone else sees what you see or not. You're believing in the possibilities of your success, despite the unknown and regardless of any naysayers who revel in raising doubt.

What new skills have you had to learn for NM that you didn't need in your previous career?

In NM, I had to develop the skill of coaching others, and being the person who's OK with not being in the spotlight. In NM, our goal is to replace ourselves and let *others* shine. I had to learn how to let go of being an "RJ"—Recognition Junkie. This characteristic might serve you in the performing world, and even in the *beginning* of your NM journey, but in order to really grow, you have to learn that success is not about you, and the more you lift others up to shine, the higher you'll soar.

What skills from your previous career have helped you most in NM?

One of the best skills from performing that you can carry into NM is probably the ability to navigate massive disappointment and keep going. Continually resetting goals and maintaining your belief system in both yourself and in the profession.

Compared to your previous career, what do you most appreciate about NM?

I most appreciate the ability to create my own future, build a residual income, and be in control of my own activity—and therefore destiny. I love seeing that anyone can succeed if they're coachable and hungry. I love being able to see the positivity and the good in the world, and recognizing that the more we succeed, the more we can do for others. The contribution side of this profession is a powerful motivator.

Compared to your previous career, what have you found to be the most challenging about NM?

The hardest thing is probably wanting it more for others than they want for themselves. It's hard to invest in someone emotionally, and then be disappointed by what people say they're going to do, but don't deliver on. It's also difficult that since you don't own the company, you have to roll with the punches if your company makes decisions along the way that you don't agree with. You have to reframe and regroup and formulate a "spin" and just *go on*, because you have to align yourself with it…or get off the boat!

What do you consider to be the most important factor to achieving success in NM?

Success in NM can be an elusive thing but it always helps to have a positive outlook. Be massively consistent in your activity levels whether you feel like it or not, and find that moment when you need to step up and become a leader instead of just a follower. If you always just follow, you'll never become like the leaders you admire. Overall, you have to find joy in the journey, managing your disappointments along the way.

What advice would you give to someone coming into NM with a background similar to yours?

It's a way to create a stable, residual income that comes in whether you work or not. It's a way to put in the work now to support your dreams in the future. By investing even a small, but consistent amount of time in your business, you can be in control of your own financial future. With an extra $$$$ a month, the amount of choices you'll have in life and the amount of time you'll have to devote to your other passions will certainly grow or even become unlimited.

Treat it like a business and apply the same principles that make you keep auditioning. No one goes to two auditions in NYC and gives up! So why do people do this in network marketing? You need to have a vision, go after it, believe in yourself, put your best foot forward whether you feel like it or not, be your best you, do something towards your goals every day, never quit on a bad day, and go after your dreams. You already have all the same traits you need to succeed if you're already a performer, so read personal development, learn as much as you can about becoming a network marketing professional, and go after it today! It'll change your life.

POLICE OFFICER AND FEDERAL CROWN ATTORNEY COMPARED TO A FLIP FLOP CEO®
PAMELA BARNUM
Police Officer/Federal Crown Attorney

What have you found to be the biggest differences between your previous career and NM?

- My previous career as a Federal Crown Attorney was very scheduled and lacked flexibility. I worked very long days and my personal life always took a backseat to my career.

- Network marketing is dedicated to you being true to you—you don't have to be a clone of everyone else. As a lawyer, being different or "marching to the beat of your own drum" is discouraged. In network marketing, it's encouraged. You are encouraged to be the best you!

- Building your career around your life instead of the other way around is a huge difference. As a lawyer, everything I did was second to my career. As a network marketer, I have the freedom to build my business around my life— anywhere, anytime. That's my favorite part!

- Income levels are not set in network marketing; there is no glass ceiling. As a lawyer, I could only earn money for the hours I worked and there are only so many hours in a day. As a network marketer, I am paid on my sales volume, not on the hours worked. There is no limit to the amount of money I can earn.

- Zero discrimination. Although women have achieved a lot in terms of gender equality, there is still much to be done. Network marketing does not discriminate based on your gender, age, education, seniority, experience, geographical location, or anything else. You're paid for your performance and the performance of the team you lead. The more you grow yourself and help others achieve their goals, the more income you can earn as a network marketer.

What things are the same in your previous career and NM?

- Being a "people person" is very important in both careers. If you don't enjoy working with people, you will find this career very challenging. I also learned a lot about people when I worked as an undercover police officer for eight of my twelve policing years.

- Time management skills are critical in both careers. Although my schedule was given to me when I worked as a lawyer, I learned how valuable time is. As a network marketer, I set my own schedule using some of the time-management skills I learned as a lawyer.

What new skills have you had to learn for NM that you didn't need in your previous career?

- Personal development is encouraged and accessible with network marketing. My previous career as a lawyer was focused around my ability to argue cases, understand the law, and communicate with witnesses. Who I was as a person was not relevant as a lawyer. As a network marketer, the opposite is true. Who I am as a person is very relevant and often the determining factor in my success. I've leaned that helping people on their personal growth journey is critically important to my success as a network marketer.

What skills from your previous career have helped you most in NM?

- Understanding different personality types and knowing how to communicate effectively with them.

- Being organized. This has served me very well in my career as a professional network marketer. I am able to demonstrate effective time-management skills that enable people to build their business in the pockets of their time. Everyone is busy—there is no disputing that. Being organized helps you focus on the income-producing activities that will help you build your business and change more lives.

Compared to your previous career, what do you most appreciate about NM?

- The "people first" mantra that the profession has. Encouraging people to dream again and providing them with the tools to achieve their goals.

Compared to your previous career, what have you found to be the most challenging about NM?

- Ironically it is the same thing I love about both: the people. Because I have such a passion for network marketing—a deep-seated belief that it can help people reach their goals—I often want it more for them than they want it for themselves. Believing in people when they do not believe in themselves can be challenging.

What do you consider to be the most important factor to achieving success in NM?

The most important factor is that they **CARE**.

C they are Coachable and open to learning success strategies

A they are Available—People must set time aside to build their business; success will not show up if you don't.

R they are Reliable—If they say they are going to do something (make a call, attend an event, or connect with people), they need to do it. How can you attract people into your business if you're not prepared to show up yourself?

E they are Enthusiastic / energetic - People buy you and what you stand for, not the products. They want to connect with you; they want what you have. If you aren't excited or enthusiastic about your products and business, how can you expect anyone else to be?

What advice would you give to someone coming into NM with a background similar to yours?

- Be open to looking at things from a different perspective. Continuing to do what you've always done will get you the same results you've always gotten. You can bring your professional credentials to the table and use those to help others and help yourself. Let go of the attachment to your title, to the letters behind your name, and be open to the opportunity that exists with network marketing. You don't have to do it full time, you can do it part time and keep your current career if you want to. The options are unlimited. The flexibility is unparalleled, and the ability to help more people and change more lives is unbeatable.

HUMAN RESOURCES COMPARED TO A FLIP FLOP CEO®

EILEEN WILLIAMS
Human Resources

What have you found to be the biggest differences between your previous career and NM?

The biggest difference—and really the greatest gift—is the importance of personal development. In NM, the more you work on yourself, the better your results. In HR, your role is of course to serve others and protect the company. In NM, we have an opportunity to be an entrepreneur which means we have complete freedom in what we choose to do. Freedom was the main reason I joined NM.

What things are the same in your previous career and NM?

You wouldn't think this, but HR and NM are very similar. The skills used are the same: leadership and training development, recruitment, coaching, team building, and mentorship. The motivation to help others and mentor others to succeed is similar in both professions. My passion for helping people succeed is applicable to both professions, but in NM, I own my results 100%.

What new skills have you had to learn for NM that you didn't need in your previous career?

The most important lesson—not sure if it is a skill—is the ability to exercise faith.

The biggest skill I had to learn was how to speak in front of large groups of people and inspire them with my words. This was not needed in HR.

What skills from your previous career have helped you most in NM?

Coaching, mentoring, and leadership development have been the most important skills. The ability to develop relationships and support people at all levels of their development has been vital.

Compared to your previous career, what do you most appreciate about NM?

I appreciate that I am 100% responsible for my future and completely own my business. This ownership has given me personal empowerment and the ability to invest in myself and reap the rewards of that.

Compared to your previous career, what have you found to be the most challenging about NM?

The biggest challenge in NM is that you have to exercise *faith* every moment of every day. When you work for a company, the structure allows you to fall back on that structure as your support. In NM, you truly can create what you want and the only limitation is yourself. I love that the most.

What do you consider to be the most important factor to achieving success in NM?

I would rephrase this question to "long-term success" with NM. The most important factor is the powerful laws of the universe, one of them being the law of cause and effect. Always do the right thing, because you will get back what you put out.

What advice would you give to someone coming into NM with a background similar to yours?

Embrace the fact that your passion is to help people and serve others. There is no greater profession than NM if you want to help others make the most of their lives. By helping others, you will help yourself and have a positive impact on the world.

NURSE PRACTITIONER COMPARED TO A FLIP FLOP CEO®

AMY CASSIDY
Nurse Practitioner

What have you found to be the biggest differences between your previous career and NM?

I discovered the biggest difference between my career and network marketing about six months into my NM business. As a nurse practitioner, I did my very best for my patients. But, ultimately, the disease or the injury determined their fate. I could intervene as much as medically and prayerfully as possible, but I always had a healthy perspective that I was not in 100% control of the outcome.

In my NM business, I had a contradictory perspective. I felt the success of every consultant who enrolled under me was A. 100% up to me, and B. 100% in my control. HA! I have to laugh at that now in retrospect. I don't know why I started in NM with this assumption. That certainly wasn't how I perceived my sponsor. I didn't feel like she was responsible for my success, but for whatever reason, it would kill me to see my consultants flounder, fail, or quit completely. I took a lot of that burden on myself. Now, nearly three years later, I realize it's actually very similar to my previous career. I can intervene, train, coach, and lead the horse to water, but I can't make her drink.

What things are the same in your previous career and NM?

My passion in life is helping people. Being a nurse practitioner satisfied that passion, because I worked with the sick and injured every day. Doing my best to help them get well and leave the hospital better than when they came in. NM allows me to fulfill this passion as well. I'm able to help people to reach their financial goals, business goals, and just life goals in general. The word, "goals" could be easily interchangeable with, "dreams." Although, the latter may seem cheesy. But, it's true, nonetheless.

What new skills have you had to learn for NM that you didn't need in your previous career?

Leadership is a skill I have had to learn and develop as I grow my NM business. As a nurse practitioner, I worked as a team member with a common goal to make a person well. In NM, as I grow a team of now thousands of people, I realize I need to help lead them to the same success I have. I feel partly responsible for their success, even though, in reality, it's up to them to do the work to succeed. Being a leader of a large team of fellow network marketers is something I'm continually developing, and is something I thought I would never be cut out to do. I most certainly want to lead by example, and in turn, create leaders who are capable of growing teams of their own.

What skills from your previous career have helped you most in NM?

Gaining trust immediately in a relationship. With my patients, I had to introduce myself and establish a trusting relationship immediately, either with them, or with their family members. Walking into a room and convincing someone I was capable of saving their life was no easy task, and it took a few years to develop. The same goes with talking with people about my network marketing business. There's a natural defensive wall that arises when I'm speaking with a prospect about my business, and I need to draw on my skills to establish a trusting relationship first, before we can proceed with a business relationship. They need to trust me, otherwise we won't be able to move forward to success together.

Compared to your previous career, what do you most appreciate about NM?

The time freedom. 100%. I came from a world of 12-hour shifts under the fluorescent lights of hospital hallways. Nights, weekends, holidays, my children's birthdays. My life revolved around my work schedule. In NM, I live my life and fit in the work around it. That's what I appreciate the most. I'm free to truly live my life. In my previous career, I was with countless patients as they were drawing their final breaths. They all wanted the same thing at the end of their lives: to have had more time with the ones they loved. I knew this was something

I had to find for myself and my family. And I found it in NM.

Compared to your previous career, what have you found to be the most challenging about NM?

Honestly, it has been overcoming the stigma of NM. It truly is an incredible business model that, given the right company, can bring the financial and time freedom that so many people are desperately seeking, but are keeping their options limited by not even considering NM.

What do you consider to be the most important factor to achieving success in NM?

Consistency. I think people expected me to quit in the beginning. I had a great career, I was well-respected, well-paid, and would eventually see the light and quit that silly, little NM business. And then I didn't. I kept growing that silly, little business. It grew so large that I was able to leave the medical field, as I had matched my six-figure income as a nurse practitioner. And then it continued to grow, and I continued to actively and publicly work my NM business. And with that consistency came credibility. That this was a real thing. That it wasn't going anywhere, and that I was continuing to stand behind it.

What advice would you give to someone coming into NM with a background similar to yours?

Go for it. Find a NM company that you resonate with, and sign up. We already have a large network of intelligent individuals. They appreciate business and numbers, and are probably just as curious as you are to finding out if there really is "a better way." That there is a way to break free from the 12-hour shifts and human excrement (well, that is, if you don't have children). That network of people in your current career will be a resource and a launching pad for your NM business. Find a company with a product that would be appealing to your network. You have already developed so many of the skills necessary to be successful in a NM business, you just have to put yourself out there and give it a try!

SONG WRITER COMPARED TO A FLIP FLOP CEO®

SUE SHIFRIN-CASSIDY
Song Writer, Entertainer

What have you found to be the biggest differences between your previous career and NM?

The most glaring difference for me is the fact that NM is a career that requires you to help others become successful in order for you to achieve success. That certainly was not the case in my former profession. The music business requires a person to be extremely territorial and competitive. I was threatened by people who were also striving to secure that one open slot on a record. I was always looking over my shoulder—who was more talented, more connected, worked harder, was "luckier"? Now those are the very qualities I am looking for in other people!

What things are the same in your previous career and NM?

NM requires hard work. It requires learning the industry and the skills to become successful. Every business does. In NM, you're your own boss, so doing this business was easier for me than for someone who is used to being an employee in the corporate world. Also, start-up costs are very low.

What new skills have you had to learn for NM that you didn't need in your previous career?

I have learned new people skills. In the music business, I worked mostly on my own. I relied on myself for my success. I didn't have "a village" that supported me or I could trust and support in return. I have learned to be more generous of my time and spirit through personal development and I have learned how to duplicate myself by adhering to the higher principles of NM.

What skills from your previous career have helped you most in NM?

I developed a strong work ethic in the music business. I learned how to be my own boss and how to be disciplined. I realized that if it was meant to be it was going to be up to me. Every day, I went into the recording studio and worked crazy long hours—most times without reward. I kept going and learning and growing as a songwriter, whether a song got recorded and made me money, or not. I never quit; I still write music without having any guarantee of success!

Compared to your previous career, what do you most appreciate about NM?

Similarly to the music business, I love having ownership of a business where I choose to work my own hours and where I can live my life on my own terms. But, mostly, I appreciate having a "family" of people who I love and support and who offer that right back to me. I am beyond blessed to have this sense of belonging that I never experienced in the music business or anywhere else.

Compared to your previous career, what have you found to be the most challenging about NM?

Honestly, realizing how simple it is to do NM. I didn't say it's easy...I said simple. As a creative person, I really had to understand that I needed to follow the system that was already in place. For me, I had to constantly remind myself to just follow that system and to not try to reinvent the wheel.

What do you consider to be the most important factor to achieving success in NM?

Never give anyone else a crystal ball for your life. No one has a crystal ball. If your heart leads you into this profession, follow it and trust yourself to know what is best for you. Treat this like a business and not a hobby. Treat this business like getting on a plane: lock the door, commit to staying on the ride, and don't get off until you land where you want.

What advice would you give to someone coming into NM with a background similar to yours?

Jump in with both feet! There's nothing to lose. NM can be your insurance policy—your security—in a very insecure profession. Your NM business can pay you while you are still writing songs, and could even become an income stream to help you do all kinds of creative things like make your own album, direct or produce a film, or even take a musical to Broadway!

NATUROPATHIC PHYSICIAN COMPARED TO A FLIP FLOP CEO®

JOHN NEUSTADT, ND
Naturopathic Physician, Entrepreneur

What have you found to be the biggest differences between your previous career and NM?

The most significant difference is the business model itself. Medicine is a fee-for-service business. I was only paid for the hours I worked. And if I didn't work for whatever reason—if I was injured or decided to take a vacation with my family—my income would stop. That was a constant source of stress and worry. And if I wanted to increase my income, I'd have to work more hours, hire more people, and assume more overhead, which would add even more stress to my life and leave even less time for my family, myself, and the things I loved most.

But with network marketing, my wife and I have freed ourselves from the billable hour by creating residual income. Every time someone purchases our company's products from us or one of our business partners, we earn a commission on that sale. And since people are predictably reordering our products, we can estimate what our income will be in the coming months. So when we want to take a vacation, we don't worry about losing income. In fact, since meeting new people is an essential part of this gig, vacations are actually great for our business. We've met folks while traveling who have become customers and business partners.

Network marketing has also freed me from geographical constraints, where I could only help people who could physically walk through my clinic doors. With our network marketing business, we've helped folks in multiple countries enjoy the benefits of our products and create incomes that have allowed them to save their homes, retire themselves or their spouses from jobs they no longer loved, pay for medical treatment, and pay it forward in time and money to causes near and dear to their hearts. That simply isn't possible in clinical medicine.

What things are the same in your previous career and NM?

Both medicine and network marketing are focused on helping others improve their lives. It's about being of service. Of finding out about the other person and seeing if we have something that could help them improve their lives. It's one of the most rewarding aspects of this business for me.

What new skills have you had to learn for NM that you didn't need in your previous career?

The greatest skill I've acquired is how to connect with someone in a less formal way than in clinical medicine.

There's an implicit dynamic that exists in the patient-doctor relationship. The patient comes in and the doctor is the expert to whom the patient is turning for help. But with network marketing, people aren't coming to me for help with a specific issue. Instead, I had to learn how to connect with people in casual conversation to find out about them—their life situation, not simply their health. The process of building rapport and trust is very different in network marketing. Most people don't connect the dots on their own about how network marketing could help them. So it's our job to help them see the potential benefits. In medicine, the potential benefits were very clear. They were sick. I gave them my recommendation and they either followed it or they didn't. But with network marketing, they might not immediately see the benefits, so instead of telling them what to do as I did in medicine (prescribing a treatment), I had to learn a more subtle approach and simply ask if they'd be interested in taking a look at what we're doing to see if it might be a good fit.

What skills from your previous career have helped you most in NM?

Listening and asking questions. In medicine, it's our job to ask questions, listen carefully, and ask follow-up questions to flush out the relevant details and fully understand the patients' experiences. Those listening skills I was taught in medical school are extremely helpful in network marketing. Similar to medicine, we train our business partners to ask a question, and then be quiet. Let the other person talk, and really listen to the answer. Then ask another question. People love talking about themselves, and when you create the space for them to do so, they share a tremendous amount. And when you ask questions out of true curiosity and caring, they tend to open up and connect with you even more. Being genuinely interested in them and listening to what they're saying let's me discover if there's an aspect of our business that might be valuable to them.

Compared to your previous career, what do you most appreciate about NM?

I love the ability to make a living that allows us to truly put our family and ourselves first. In medicine, I was tied to my clinic and had to schedule my life around my work. But with network marketing, we schedule our work around our life. Because our network marketing business is a virtual business—no brick and mortar, no inventory to track and deliver, no employees to manage—we're able to work anywhere we have cell service and wifi. We both work from home, or our favorite coffee shop, or wherever we happen to be. We've had calls with prospects from a chair lift in Utah. We've worked with our team from a beach in Bora Bora. And what excites us most now about this business is how we're able to help others create this same freedom in their lives. I couldn't do that in medicine.

Compared to your previous career, what have you found to be the most challenging about NM?

Joining an already established network marketing business was by far the most challenging. By the time I jumped in and started building our business with my wife, she'd already built a six-figure-a-month income for us. The transition from being husband and wife to side-by-side business partners posed specific challenges.

As a doctor who owned my own medical clinic and a dietary supplement company, I was used to calling the shots. I also had the arrogant idea that since I'd been watching my wife build the business for years, I knew what the business needed and could come in and make changes to make it even better. If I'd been more humble, it would have gone much smoother. As the saying goes, hindsight is 20/20.

In looking back, this is what I would've done differently: I would have recognized that my wife—as the primary NM business builder—was the expert, and I was just like any other newbie. She was the CEO, and I wish I'd asked her what she thought the business needed and where my skills might be helpful. I would have let her completely guide me. While I did go through our new business partner training that we put our other new partners through—and I actively starting recruiting, training, and working with consultants—I made the mistake of telling her what improvements I thought the business needed before I fully understood it. Instead of faithfully following the business system and example of my wife, I thought I'd come in and make my mark by improving a proven system. Boy was I arrogant. But we worked through all that and now we both bring our specific strengths to the table and work very well together.

What do you consider to be the most important factor to achieving success in NM?

Hands down the most important factor in achieving success is mindset. This business requires sustained effort. It's not get rich quick. And developing an attitude that you'll be successful no matter what is indispensable. This way of thinking requires people to commit to doing their best, understand that they will make mistakes along the way, but that they'll learn from those mistakes and keep making improvements to get better every day. It's also important to have the fundamental belief that we're all worthy of being wildly successful and that if we'll put everything we have into developing ourselves personally and professionally, we can grow into the best versions of ourselves and design the life we really want to live.

What advice would you give to someone coming into NM with a background similar to yours?

My best advice is to lean on your upline sponsor for guidance, plug into your company's training, and follow the business system. Just like medical school teaches healthcare providers a way to think and practice medicine, your network marketing company has its own system that will teach you how to do this business. Medicine is about studying, studying, studying, and then finally—after you've studied enough and passed exams—you start earning a living. When you finally get into clinical practice, you're an expert who has spent years honing your craft before you start getting paid.

Network marketing, however, is an earn-as-you-learn business. You won't spend years studying before you launch your business, and you won't feel like an expert when you start talking to people. The only way to become comfortable in this business is by doing it. Those who keep reading everything they can and don't do the fundamental activity required to build a business—talking to people—are getting ready to get ready. Pushing through any discomfort or fear, and putting yourself out there and talking to people, is the only way to become an expert and grow this sucker. Follow your company's proven system and it will make the transition from novice to expert easier and faster.

ENGINEER COMPARED TO A FLIP FLOP CEO®

DARRYL ICE
Engineer and Business Operations Manager
for Fortune 500 Global Manufacturing
Company

What have you found to be the biggest differences between your previous career and NM?

There are no employees. I'm in control of my schedule, and it's as flexible as I want it to be. But there's a general lack of understanding of what we do.

What things are the same in your previous career and NM?

Value of leadership, casting a vision, and empowering people to succeed.

What new skills have you had to learn for NM that you didn't need in your previous career?

I've learned to motivate people to start their own business, and I've gained knowledge about my company's products.

What skills from your previous career have helped you most in NM?

Leadership, relating to people, and understanding the traditional channel to market and how to contrast that with NM.

Compared to your previous career, what do you most appreciate about NM?

Ability to help people regardless of background/experience,

flexibility, independence, and efficient and effective channel to market.

Compared to your previous career, what have you found to be the most challenging about NM?

Employees will work hard to keep their job. In NM, many people will not put forth the same effort. Too many people are looking for a quick buck, and many not willing to set goals and think long term.

What do you consider to be the most important factor to achieving success in NM?

Self-motivated individuals who have the ability to create a long-term vision and set goals, willingness to handle rejection, and to stick to a simple, repeatable system that people can understand.

What advice would you give to someone coming into NM with a background similar to yours?

Be willing to think long term. Don't simply compare compensation plans; place a value on your time and lifestyle when deciding. Get a good understanding of why you want to create passive income, create a vision of what this will do for you in the future, and use this to keep you motivated.

CO-FOUNDER/OWNER OF A BIO-TECH COMPANY COMPARED TO A FLIP FLOP CEO

DR. GARY LINDNER, PHD
Reproductive Physiologist, Co-founder/
owner Bio-Technology Company

What have you found to be the biggest differences between your previous career and NM?

Recruiting people for their reasons, not mine. In my previous career, I would hire professionals or experienced individuals to leverage their talents to make our company more profitable. In network marketing, you're looking for people who want more money, more time freedom, and more balance in their lives. They join you for their reasons. It's paramount to have relevant conversations to know what they want and how you can help them achieve it.

What things are the same in your previous career and NM?

As an employer in my traditional business role, or as a leader in my network marketing business, it's our responsibility to train, support, and empower our new people to have the greatest chance of success in achieving their goals. Different subject matter and techniques, but very similar overall principles apply in both models.

What new skills have you had to learn for NM that you didn't need in your previous career?

I've had to train myself to be a better listener and ask more questions (believe me…not an easy task for an owner and employer with decades in their field/business and or business), and I am no exception in this case. Being a good listener is paramount to successful enrollment of others in your network marketing business, and critical to empowering them as leaders to achieve their individual success.

In my traditional role as a business owner, I talked more, listened less, and gave more directives instead of suggestions, asked fewer questions, and gave more orders to employees. I fully appreciate, in retrospect, that being a better listener would have immeasurably helped me be a better employer, better business owner, and better friend to those who I employed. I have learned many aspects of business in my network marketing experience that are directly applicable to any traditional business.

What skills from your previous career have helped you most in NM?

My skills as an educator and trainer for my students and employees has directly transferred over into my network marketing business. I've also noticed that people with a teaching background or experience have an easier transition into the network marketing business model. All we need to do is empower individuals with some relatively simple skills to master. These include contacting, creating interest, inviting, one on one (or three person conversations or presentations), and follow up.

My previous position allowed me the opportunity to work globally. This has been very valuable personally, and has helped others on our team expand their businesses to other countries. A better understanding of cultures, business practices, and personalities in other countries can be very beneficial in expanding globally, if your network marketing company is an international company.

Compared to your previous career, what do you most appreciate about NM?

The residual income aspect of network marketing, and the way it has expanded my time freedom exponentially, is the advantage that I most appreciate. I have spent most of my business career as self-employed or as a business owner. That has afforded me the autonomy to control my own schedule, choose who I work with, and create some time freedom. Network marketing has amplified those very desirable characteristics that I value so much. That is precisely why I was drawn to the business model. Network marketing gives any of us the opportunity to create income without our physical presence.

My previous career required my physical presence to perform services, and a great deal of travel both domestically and internationally was involved in our operational functions. At great expense to my health, my family and friendships, I came to an epiphany that maybe there were other things I could do to help others and generate income. I really didn't consider network marketing to be the solution, but through a series of occurrences, I found my answer truly was network marketing. The ability to use the internet to create interest and provide information, as well as other real-time technological resources, has eliminated much of the travel involved in our network marketing business.

Compared to your previous career, what have you found to be the most challenging about NM?

The most challenging aspect of network marketing is maintaining motivation for individuals on your team. We all have slow times and inconvenient times that are not conducive to building our businesses. This is an issue in smaller teams with only a few individuals or that lack a leader to help the entire team grow. It's much easier to motivate a committed team, rather than just a few individuals. The underlying beauty of network marketing is that its success is team based, not individually based. The more we empower others to get what they want, the more we get what we want in return. Very true, not only in network marketing, but in life in general.

Another challenge is that people don't know or perceive they need what you have to offer. Many times they make decisions without first being informed. Something they heard from a friend or family member without substantiation is often enough for them to make a rash decision. That is why being a good listener and addressing concerns is paramount to success in any business, but even more important in network marketing, where so many clichés and misinformation is present. That's the value intended by the wonderful authors of this book and why I have elected to be a small part of this information process.

What do you consider to be the most important factor to achieving success in NM?

Persistence as with any endeavor of value is paramount. I have seen many give up because their network marketing business didn't meet their initial expectations. Building a strong team takes time and a consistent work effort. One of the most beneficial aspects of network marketing is that it can be done successfully with part-time effort, as long as that effort is consistent. It is repetition of simple activities that lead to success. The law called gestation states: things take a set amount of time to grow. What many may consider an "overnight success" has been many months or years in creation.

What advice would you give to someone coming into NM with a background similar to yours?

My advice is don't pre-judge an opportunity before you have fully investigated it. Use sound business evaluations to make your decision and avoid emotional decisions. Investigate the company, its financial solvency, its officers, their product line, and leadership in the field. Choose a company that has more than just a good product and compensation plan. Look for one you can be passionate about, and can share their mission and vision with integrity. Choose the one that best suits your strengths and ideals. I highly suggest a thorough due diligence of any opportunity is a worthwhile endeavor.

LUXURY HOME REAL ESTATE SPECIALIST COMPARED TO A FLIP FLOP CEO®

LOREN ROBIN
Real Estate (Luxury Home Specialist)

What have you found to be the biggest differences between your previous career and NM?

While selling real estate, I was on call 24/7/365. I did not own my life. Network marketing has given me time and financial freedom. I can pick and choose who I want to build my business with, and who I spend time with.

What things are the same in your previous career and NM?

Mastering the art of building and nurturing long-term relationships is exactly the same. It's all about the relationship and referrals.

What new skills have you had to learn for NM that you didn't need in your previous career?

The areas where I've learned the most are leadership and personal development. In order to grow your business in network marketing, you must improve your listening skills, communication skills, and truly be able to connect with people. It's similar in the real estate profession, but NM is a much larger platform with the ability to impact mass numbers of people.

What skills from your previous career have helped you most in NM?

My vision. My ability to be rejection proof. My communications skills and work ethic.

Compared to your previous career, what do you most appreciate about NM?

The peaceful and calm feeling I have knowing my income is residual. I don't feel pressured all the time to go out and sell another house to pay the bills.

Compared to your previous career, what have you found to be the most challenging about NM?

Getting a prospect to catch the vision. Getting new Reps to understand that you do not make very much money your first couple of years, but when you do start making money, it's residual and powerful.

What do you consider to be the most important factor to achieving success in NM?

Believing in the industry, your company and, most of all, yourself.

What advice would you give to someone coming into NM with a background similar to yours?

Leverage your relationships. Prospect highly successful people who feel dissatisfied with what they're doing. Lead by example. Make people want what you have.

RV DEALERSHIP OWNER COMPARED TO A FLIP FLOP CEO®

CHRIS WEILERT
RV Dealership Owner

What have you found to be the biggest differences between your previous career and NM?

The ability to leverage time, and the opportunity to create a true residual income. My company sold RV's, so sales were "one, and done, and onto selling the next one", constantly. Overhead was massive. NM's overhead is simply the norm of everyday spending habits. To rid myself of a six-figure-a-month overhead was a tremendous burden of stress that was lifted.

What things are the same in your previous career and NM?

The ability to simply connect with people. I truly believe people miss that touch of interaction with one another. I love talking and connecting with people, and I always try to add humor in a conversation—people listen and learn more when they're engaged with humor and laughter.

What new skills have you had to learn for NM that you didn't need in your previous career?

I learned to have more patience with people and to understand the process of building a team of consultants. The NM industry has a "timing" effect that is really different; it's not always the right "time" for someone to get involved when we want them to. Patience is important; some people jump in right away, and some people join you months or years later because they might need some time of proof! I needed it.

What skills from your previous career have helped you most in NM?

People skills and organizational skills. With my previous company, I had to wear a lot of hats—from sales, finance, time management, social media, public relations, etc. In NM, we also have to wear a lot of hats. I think the balance helps.

Compared to your previous career, what do you most appreciate about NM?

Time freedom it can create is most important to us. We now have two children. I was at my dealership pretty much every day. I took off maybe two days a month, and with NM I'm able to be home and schedule my work after I schedule my life with my boys. Biggest gift about NM is that we can create wealth. Wealth is not about being rich; you can have money and work non-stop and become rich, but creating wealth is about becoming smarter with your business and having actually time.

Compared to your previous career, what have you found to be the most challenging about NM?

To be completely honest and transparent, some people are not cut out for our industry. It's ownership of being a true entrepreneur. It's about the short-term sacrifice for the long-term gift. I understand everyone needs "right now money," we all do, but seeds take time to grow and not everyone has that vision or patience. If I told you, "You could make over $100k in NM in your first two years, but you might only make $8-10k your first year, would you stick it out?" Most won't, and then when success is not given, sometimes our industry gets put into another category which can create a bad stigma—that upsets me. We are business owners, and building empires will take years, not weeks or months. It's interesting how people sometimes create this "other" category they think NM fits in. In the next five years, I guarantee that one out of four households will be using some type of product or service from NM.

What do you consider to be the most important factor to achieving success in NM?

Treat it like a true business. It takes years to build, not months. Stay the course and follow people whose businesses you want, or want to be at that level. Don't follow people who are struggling in this industry and on the verge to jump to their 6th company. Stay with one and make it work long term. Again, patience and planting seeds takes time. People can come and go on your teams, but you need to always *stay* and *show* the way.

What advice would you give to someone coming into NM with a background similar to yours?

It can honestly be a very different world, but it really boils down to how your treat people and how you connect with people. Connect with people and listen. It's sales, but in my opinion it's no pressure. We're simply showing people how to redirect their spending habits they already do on a daily basis. It's easy; don't make it hard.

ADDITIONAL RESOURCES
WE RECOMMEND

THESE ARE SOME OF THE BOOKS, CDS, WEBSITES AND PEOPLE THAT WE LOVE. WE THINK YOU'LL LOVE THEM TO.

Building Belief in Network Marketing

- *The Flip Flop CEO®*, Lory Muirhead, Janine Finney, Whitney Roberts
- *Dare to Dream and Work to Win*, Dr. Tom Barrett
- *Success Happens*, Dr. Tom Barrett
- *The 45 Second Presentation That Will Change Your Life*, Don Failla
- *The Four Year Career*, Richard Bliss Brooke
- *Brilliant Compensation CD*, Tim Sales
- *The Business School for People Who Like Helping People*, Robert Kiyosake and Sharon Lechter

Choosing a Company and Products to Represent

- Direct Selling Association, www.DSA.org

Developing Professional Network Marketing Skills

- *Go Pro 7 Steps to Becoming A Network Marketing Professional,* Eric Worre
- Networking Times Magazine (NetworkingTimes.com)
- *Best Worst First*, Margie Aliprandi and Martha Finney
- *7 Habits of Highly Effective Network Marketing Professionals,* Stephen R. Covey